A CRUCIBLE OF NATIONS

THE GEOPOLITICS OF THE CAUCASUS

BY LAUREN GOODRICH AND PETER ZEIHAN

WITH CONCLUSION BY GEORGE FRIEDMAN

STRATFOR
GLOBAL INTELLIGENCE

STRATFOR
221 W. 6th Street, Suite 400
Austin, TX 78701

Printed in the United States of America

ISBN: 1461109426
EAN-13: 9781461109426

Publisher: Grant Perry
Editor: Robin Blackburn
Project Coordinator: Robert Inks
Designer: TJ Lensing

CONTENTS

ILLUSTRATIONS

ILLUSTRATIONS

INTRODUCTION

In the Caucasus, three great historical empires converge: Russia, Persia and Turkey. They are no longer empires but republics, and Persia has changed its name to Iran, while Russia called itself the Soviet Union for seven decades. The names, ideologies and fortunes have changed, but these three great powers have this in common: Each is part of the Caucasus region but has greater interests outside the Caucasus region. That means that interests far away frequently drive the behavior of the three great powers in the Caucasus. For all three powers, the Caucasus is sometimes at the center of their thinking and sometimes an afterthought.

Another characteristic they share is that all three are rising powers. Turkey is shaking off three generations of self-imposed isolation and exploring its neighborhood. The process is awkward, painful and plagued with mistakes and setbacks, but Ankara is tired of having its fate determined by others and so has no choice but to continue. Iran seeks to reach into the areas near it that have been weakened by the Soviet collapse and the U.S. wars in the Islamic world. Alone among the region's states in its relative internal and external security, Iran has many opportunities for expansion. The post-Soviet collapse is over, and Russia's twilight will not begin for another decade, producing a rising tide of Russian power throughout its periphery that seems irresistible — until it recedes. The attention of all three powers shifts based on the demands of the day, but all regularly cross gazes in the Caucasus. If they do not cross swords there, it will be a rare exception to an ancient rule.

The are also three nations entirely within the Caucasus that are much smaller and weaker than those great powers: Armenia, Azerbaijan and Georgia. They are ancient mountain cultures that have survived because the rugged mountains provided natural barriers to invaders. During the last century, Czarist Russia, and then the Soviet Union, occupied all three nations. The Russians changed borders, moved populations and forced cultural changes but were unable to suppress the Caucasus peoples' national self-awareness. Indeed, in odd ways, these mountain cultures fought back by giving in. The Caucasus nations played Politburo politics with the same ruthless cunning with which they fought each other. The Georgians even gave the Russians Joseph Stalin.

Each Caucasus country contains fragments of the populations of the other countries in the region, and each contains smaller groups — fragments of older nations. The claims about what belongs to each of these nations and what was stolen from them date back for centuries; yesterday and a thousand years ago are remembered with equal vividness. The very antiquity of the cultures creates the most contemporary conflicts. People still die over regions whose names are barely known outside the region and are exotic to the ears of outsiders: Nagorno-Karabakh, Ossetia, Abkhazia. In a small mountainous place, where every valley has enormous value and memories are long, there is little room for compromise and little appetite for generosity.

Most Azerbaijanis, having been conquered by the Persians, live in Iran. Russia has broken Georgia's control over territory it claims. Armenia claims a blood debt against Turkey over mass murders in 1915, while Azerbaijanis claim similar debts against Armenians. This is not ancient history. Georgia fought a war with Russia in 2008, Armenians and Azerbaijanis are currently edging toward a new war, and Iranians infiltrate Azerbaijan regularly.

When all of the Caucasus is under the control of the three major powers, the region tends to be more stable than when the three smaller powers are independent. A smothering occupation limits the options for the smaller nations. When the three smaller states are independent, they attempt to purify their internal regions of smaller groups, they compete with each other and they compete with the greater powers. The friction creates both challenges and opportunities for the greater powers. Wars become seen as just another tactic in the balance-of-power game.

When STRATFOR steps back and look at the region broadly, we see a region about to trade turmoil for crisis.

We find that the Russian hold on the North Caucasus is firm, but that the challenge from Islamist and nationalist insurgents in the region is substantial and growing. There is low but increasing tension between Iran and Azerbaijan, both because northwestern Iran is ethnically Azerbaijani and that Tehran and Baku have starkly different outlooks. Turkey and Iran are sliding toward confrontation while Armenia is in indefinite confrontation with Turkey. The conflict between Armenia and Azerbaijan is almost certain to erupt into war in the near future. Russian power has broken the Georgian state, but Georgia's position makes it the logical gateway for any outside power that wishes to enter the game.

The opportunities for a range of conflicts are substantial, and the timing of such conflicts is unpredictable — and that is without factoring in the United States, whose relations with Iran, Russia and Turkey are hostile, cold and deteriorating, respectively.

This book seeks to explore how the Caucasus came to its current complications, how the rise and fall of the Persian, Turkish and Russian empires have shaped the region, and how the ascendance of all three great powers is changing the region today.

Peter Zeihan, VP, Analysis
Lauren Goodrich, Senior Eurasia Analyst
STRATFOR
Austin, Texas
May 20, 2011

GEOGRAPHY OF THE CAUCASUS

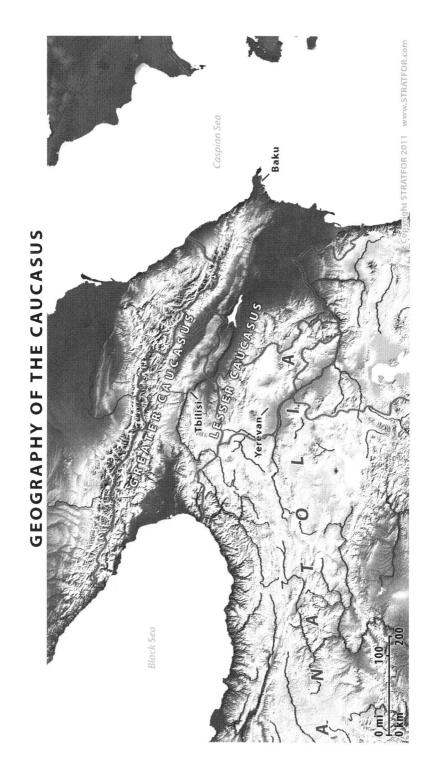

Black Sea

Caspian Sea

GREATER CAUCASUS

LESSER CAUCASUS

Tbilisi

Yerevan

Baku

0 mi   100   200
0 km

CHAPTER 1:
Physical Geography of the Caucasus Region

The Caucasus is a largely mountainous region between the Caspian and Black seas. Running from the west-northwest to the east-south-east are two parallel mountain chains: the Greater (or Northern) Caucasus and the Lesser (or Southern) Caucasus. Between the two chains are two funnel-shaped lowlands, opening toward the Black and Caspian and connecting at their narrowest point, where the Mtkvari River cuts through a small mountain chain that connects the Greater and Lesser Caucasus ranges at the modern-day city of Tbilisi. North of the Greater Caucasus the terrain quickly widens, flattens and dries, becoming the Eurasian steppe. South of the Southern Caucasus, there is no similar transformation. The Lesser Caucasus, as the name implies, are not nearly as steep or stark as the Greater Caucasus, and they soon merge with the rugged highlands of the Anatolian Plateau in the west and the Zagros Mountains in the south. The eastern of the two lowlands directly abuts the northwestern edge of Iran's Elburz Mountains.

The western portion of the Greater Caucasus is considerably higher than the eastern portion, and the vertical difference helps wring considerably more water out of air currents. Consequently, the western lowland has a humid, subtropical climate that typically receives more than 10 times more annual precipitation than the eastern lowland. This makes the western lowland more fertile, but it also generates sufficient river activity to cut myriad deep valleys into the southern flanks of the western portions of the Greater Caucasus range. This

TOPOGRAPHY OF THE WIDER REGION

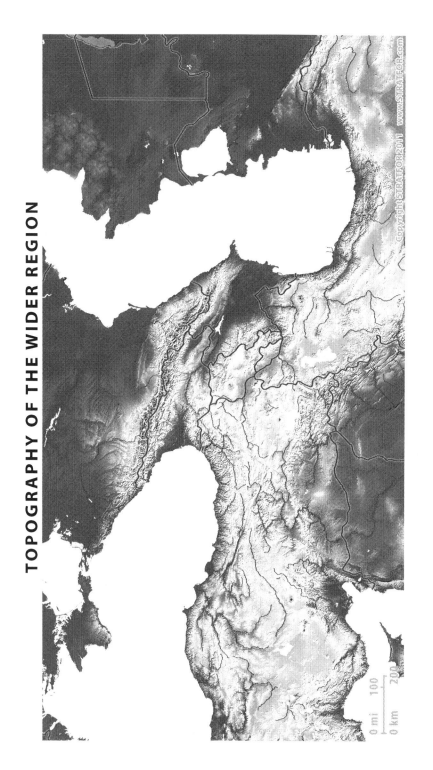

has resulted in a multitude of minority groups tucked away in western fastnesses, while the eastern plain's ethnic makeup is more unitary. Despite the western funnel's abutting the Black Sea, it is also more limited in its contact with its immediate neighbors than the eastern funnel. The coastal plains in both directions are extremely narrow — less than 2 kilometers (slightly more than 1 mile) between coast and mountain in most locations — and the southern approach does not truly widen until the Turkish Straits.

The eastern lowlands have a remarkably different climate. With most of the moisture from air currents precipitating out over the western portion of the Caucasus chains, and with the arid steppes and deserts of Central Asia just across the Caspian, the eastern lowlands have far hotter summers and far dryer winters than the western lowlands. The combination of less rainfall and lower mountains sharply curtails river activity, making the mountain borders of the eastern portions of the intra-Caucasus region much more akin to walls than the serrated valleys that dominate the western funnel. There is only one area where there is a deep cut into the Southern Caucasus — at the mountain enclave known as Nagorno-Karabakh, home of the Karabakh Armenians, who have proven most resistant to the central control of modern-day Azerbaijan.

Despite the more wall-like characteristics of the mountains in the east, the eastern flatlands are actually more exposed to the major powers to the region's north and south. The Caspian coastal plains are considerably wider and shorter than their equivalents along the Black sea, which are long and thin. Additionally, the southern portions of the eastern flatlands directly abut the Persian highlands, a region that is still quite rugged but far more accessible and traversable than the Caucasus chains.

The final piece of the region, the Armenian highlands, is not actually part of the Caucasus geography, rather being the easternmost extension of Anatolia. As such, the history of Armenia has far more in common with developments in Anatolia and Persia than it does with the Caucasus or Russia. It was not until the early 18th century that Russia began to struggle for what is now Armenia, and it was not until after World War I that the region became firmly part of the Russian sphere of influence.

The Significance of Mountains

There are very few mountainous regions of the world where STRATFOR expends much effort following events. Mountains lack navigable waterways that can be used to encourage trade — and from it, economic wealth — and the sort of broad swathes of arable land that can support large populations. The nearly invariable result is isolated, smallish, poor populations that only rarely affect events beyond their immediate territories.

What mountains do afford their inhabitants is a wealth of defensive options. One can hide — and fight an invader — in forested mountains with much more success than one can in flat plains. Outside powers find simply penetrating these regions — much less constructing the infrastructure or fielding a force required to dominate them — a gargantuan task. Mountain regions are where major powers go in times of extreme power or extreme need; they are where major powers expand to (but rarely into) to anchor their own regions and provide buffers between their empires and others'. STRATFOR obviously focuses on Afghanistan, but only because the U.S. invasion and continuing involvement after the Sept. 11 attacks limits U.S. power elsewhere, not because the U.S. effort will modify Afghanistan in any meaningful way that outlasts the U.S. military's presence there.

The Andean spine, the European Alps, the African interior or the Balkan or Korean peninsulas do not demand a great deal of attention. None of them has — or will have — the characteristics required to be geopolitically dynamic without outside assistance. Mountains are border regions, and unlike the U.S.-Mexican, Franco-German or Russo-Ukrainian frontiers, they are not borderlands that often shift. Major states wish to put as little effort into securing them as possible and then move on to (quite often literally) greener pastures.

There are two exceptions to this rule. First, Persia — modern-day Iran — is the world's only example of a mountain culture that has

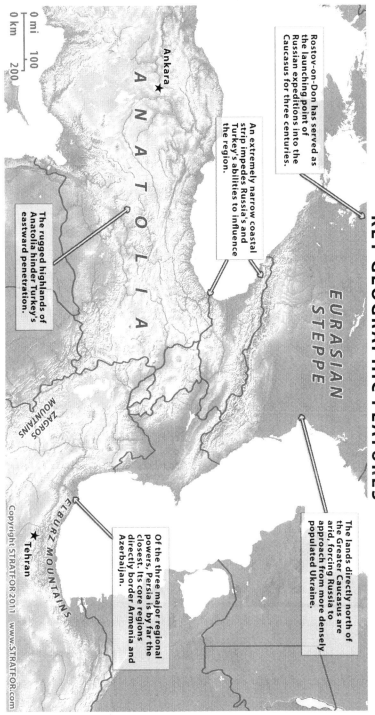

KEY GEOGRAPHIC FEATURES

Rostov-on-Don has served as the launching point of the Russian expeditions into the Caucasus for three centuries.

An extremely narrow coastal strip impedes Russia's and Turkey's abilities to influence the region.

The rugged highlands of Anatolia hinder Turkey's eastward penetration.

The lands directly north of the Greater Caucasus are arid, forcing Russia to approach from more densely populated Ukraine.

Of the three major regional powers, Persia is by far the closest. Its core regions directly border Armenia and Azerbaijan.

ANATOLIA

EURASIAN STEPPE

ZAGROS MOUNTAINS

ELBURZ MOUNTAINS

Ankara

Tehran

0 mi   100   200
0 km

Copyright STRATFOR 2011   www.STRATFOR.com

evolved into a major power. As such, STRATFOR considers Iran in a considerably different light from other major powers.

Second, mountain regions matter a great deal when great powers struggle over their orientation. Mountain peoples — who compete with each other just as vigorously as they defend themselves from outsiders — have their own geopolitics to consider. The intermingling of such grand and petit geopolitical factors makes mountain struggles fiercer and more complicated than similar struggles over less-rugged regions.

Were STRATFOR in existence during the European era, we would have been gripped with every small event that occurred in the Balkans, just as Korea would draw our gaze if this were the immediate post-World War II years. But for 2011, our attention is on the Caucasus; not only are three would-be great powers struggling over the territory, one of those powers is none other than mountainous Persia.

What the Caucasus Is — and Is Not

In describing what the Caucasus is, it is important to clarify what it is not. A glance at a map indicates that the region is an easily traversable barrier — a little more than 1,100 kilometers (650 miles) from west to east, with contiguous lowlands between the Caucasus' northern and southern chains — between the Black and Caspian seas. However, this is not the case.

First, the interior of the Caucasus has only rarely been under a single political authority, complicating any crossing. The multitude of mountain populations threatens any transport even if arrangements can be made with the rulers of the flatlands linking the Caspian and the Black seas. Second, there are no significant trade destinations within 2,000 kilometers to the region's northeast and east, raising the question of why anyone would want to cross it in the first place rather than taking safer and less politically complicated routes.

Third, the Caspian Sea is landlocked, and most of its eastern shore ranges from arid to desert, offering few trade options for any power on the sea. Fourth, the Black Sea is almost entirely landlocked; only the Turkish Straits offer egress to the wider world, making any trade route using the Caucasus completely dependent on the political authority there. Fifth, the Volga River empties into the northern Caspian, and 400 kilometers from its mouth lays a short portage to the Don, allowing for a route that bypasses the Caucasus and its petit geopolitics completely for those few wishing to use the two seas. Even during the era of the Silk Road, most of the traffic went either north or south around the Caspian rather than across it.

The Caucasus is not a significant north-south trade route, either. Russia's population core lies far to the north and finds it far easier and thus more profitable to trade across the easily traversable Northern European Plain with Europe. As a mountain state, Iran engages in very little trade of any kind. Modern Iranian trade is almost exclusively limited to petroleum and the goods purchased with petroleum income. What trade the Persians have participated in traditionally has been via the Persian Gulf or directly with Anatolia and Mesopotamia.

The Caucasus' lack of use as a transport corridor somewhat simplifies STRATFOR's analysis, limiting its scope to the role the Caucasus plays as a buffer zone among the three major powers bordering it: Russia, Turkey and Persia/Iran.

MAJOR CAUCASUS RELIGIONS

Legend:
- Armenian Apostolic Orthodox
- Georgian Orthodox
- Greek Orthodox
- Shi'ism
- Sunnism
- Yezidism
- Judaism

RUSSIA

GEORGIA

ARMENIA

AZERBAIJAN

AZ.

TURKEY

IRAN

Black Sea

Caspian Sea

0 mi   100
0 km   200

Copyright STRATFOR 2011   www.STRATFOR.com

CHAPTER 2:
Religion in the Caucasus

Like most topics relating to identity in the Caucasus, religion is murky. Somewhat surprisingly, through there have been numerous clashes with religious overtones, most conflicts have ethnicity, territory, politics and strategy as their core drivers. Religion often complicates and deepens existing clashes, but in the modern era, it has only rarely been the justification for conflict.

Orthodoxy runs through the Russian-Georgian-Armenian corridor. Armenian Orthodox (Apostolic) is separate from Russian and Georgian (Eastern), though Georgian Orthodoxy originally was part of Armenia's apostolic faith until the 7th century. This may seem like splitting hairs, but it is important to understand whom each faith considers its patriarch. The Armenian Orthodox look to Constantinople (Istanbul), whereas the Georgian and Russian Orthodox look to Moscow. During the Soviet period, Russia pressured the Armenian Orthodox to join Eastern Orthodoxy, but it still did not break the ties to the higher patriarch. Moscow has long used religion to unite people through the Caucasus, Eastern Europe and Central Asia, though small differences have limited the level of influence Moscow can wield in such a way.

Islam in the Caucasus is more complex, and the mixture of Sunnis and Shia has long created tensions. Shia can be found along the historical Persian-Azerbaijani corridor and are capped by a large Sunni population leading into Dagestan. Azerbaijan is the only Shia region in all of the former Soviet Union (most Muslims in the former Soviet Union are Sunni). However, Islam has done more to unite territories than to divide them. For example, the Russian republic of Ingushetia was converted to Islam in the 19th century and then linked to its Muslim neighbor, Chechnya. Since the fall of the Soviet Union, Islam has united populations across the northern Caucasus despite their differences. Interestingly, throughout the centuries Orthodox Georgians and Russians have joined in on both sides of clashes between Muslim regions, despite religious differences.

More recently, religion has been seen as a way for foreign groups beyond Russia, Iran and Turkey to infiltrate the Caucasus. During recent wars in the northern Caucasus (mainly the First and Second Chechen Wars), Islamists and Salafist (Wahhabist) Muslims flooded into the region, where most of the Sunni communities are Sufis. These Muslims (mainly from the Arab states) came to join their "brothers" to fight against the Russians and each other, increasing the Caucasus Muslims' capabilities and the scope of radicalization in the region. However, the influx of hardline Muslims created a rift between the Muslims in the northern Caucasus, as many fought for national independence from Russia while the newer wave was interested in creating an Islamist state.

CHAPTER 3:
Turkey's Evolving View

Contrary to the conventional wisdom, Turkey traditionally has not been a Middle Eastern power; it has been a European power. The core Turkish territories are the flatlands surrounding the Sea of Marmara and the deep, wide valleys of the extreme western end of the Anatolian Peninsula. These areas are hardwired into the trade pathways that connect Europe and Asia, and the Black Sea to the Mediterranean. The logical expansion routes for Turkey have long been northwest into the Danubian Basin, north to the Crimea, southwest into the Aegean and then southeast into the Levant, in that order. Such territories grant the Turks access to vibrant economic opportunities at a minimum of military cost.

In comparison, eastern Anatolia and the Caucasus are not economically viable territories by most standards. The further east one moves in Anatolia the more rugged, dry and hostile the land becomes. Anatolia's northern coastal strip on the Black Sea is but a few kilometers wide. Few areas of the interior are arable in the traditional sense: Irrigation is required for agriculture, road/rail construction is difficult if not impossible, and the cost of moving goods and people from place to place becomes onerous. The contrast between this region and the lands of the Sea of Marmara or the Danube River could not be starker. As such, eastern Anatolia and the Caucasus represent the last lands — not the first — that the Ottoman Empire absorbed.

Simply in terms of cost-benefit, there are many good reasons why Turkey should choose not to control the Caucasus, and deciding the specific position of the border between Turkey and the Caucasus is

THE OTTOMAN EMPIRE'S EXPANSION

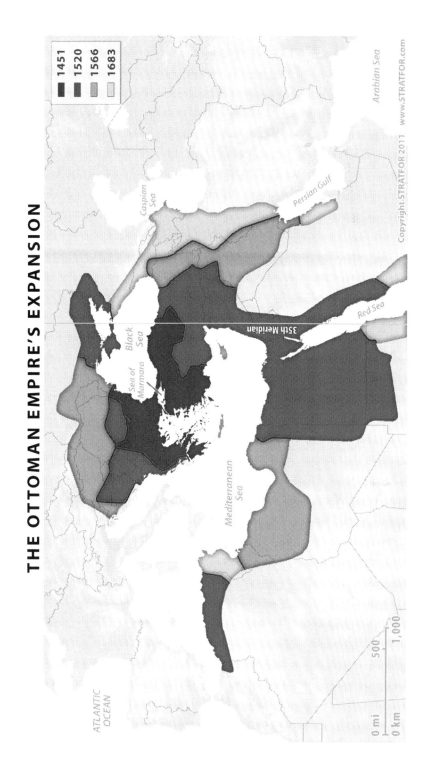

Legend:
- 1451
- 1520
- 1566
- 1683

ATLANTIC OCEAN

Caspian Sea

Arabian Sea

Persian Gulf

Black Sea

Sea of Marmara

35th Meridian

Red Sea

Mediterranean Sea

Copyright STRATFOR 2011   www.STRATFOR.com

0 mi   500   1,000
0 km

a somewhat academic exercise. The point at which Asia Minor fuses with Asia proper, just past the 35th meridian, is a reasonable place to stop. Any further and Turkey finds itself not only involved in the Caucasus' thorny affairs but also extended into a position where it is competing with the Russians and Persians directly — and is doing so far from its base of power on the western edge of Asia Minor.

This is not to say that the region is without use to the Turks, but that use has evolved considerably during the past half millennia.

During the Ottoman era, the Turks maintained forces in the region to serve as a buffer against Asiatic invaders, whether those invaders were Mongol, Arab, Persian or Russian. The fear has not been that the Caucasus would be controlled by others but instead that a power might be able to use the Caucasus as a stepping stone to the Turkish core. The Caucasus and eastern Anatolia were seen as roadblocks that a proactive Turkish force could use to painfully complicate the advance of any Asiatic power seeking battle with Istanbul.

By the beginning of World War I, this outlook was already evolving. A string of defeats in the 18th and 19th centuries had stripped the Ottoman Empire of its Danubian territories, and even in war the Turks held little hope of returning to their previous greatness. After all, the Austro-Hungarian Empire — the European power most interested in seizing former Ottoman territories in the Balkans — was technically an ally.

As the Turks' options dwindled, a centuries-old disinterest in Anatolia transformed into a competition for land and resources between the dominant Turks and the various Anatolian ethnicities. In that context, eliminating the Armenians — seen as a fifth column cooperating with the Russians — was considered paramount. Turkish and Armenian power clashed harshly throughout Anatolia in 1915 (the Turks called it a civil war, the Armenians a genocide), and by the time of the founding of the modern Turkish republic in 1923, Armenian power within the boundaries of now-Republican Turkey was no more. The post-World War I settlement also stripped the Turks of all of their lands except their Sea of Marmara core and Anatolia.

The rising importance of Anatolia to the Turkish mindset increased sharply after the World War II. Before the war, Turkey shared only its Caucasus border with the Russians. By the early Cold War years the Turks also found themselves facing off against Soviet satellite states in the Balkans and Soviet client states in the Arab world. This transformation had more than simply military implications. Turkish power rested on control of the trade routes that flowed through and across the Sea of Marmara region — maritime trade from the Danubian Basin and the Black Sea to and from the Mediterranean, and European-Asiatic land trade. With the Black Sea and Danube reduced from regional trade arteries to internal Soviet waterways, and with the Balkans and the northern tier of the Arab world entering the Russian sphere of influence, trade through the Sea of Marmara region, both land and maritime, nearly dried up completely. Turkey had no choice but to expend efforts on developing what lands it still held, as opposed to renewed imperial expansion. The result was decades of incremental development in Central Anatolia. Anatolia slowly came into its own culturally and economically and started down the long road of developing into a political complement and counterweight to the traditionally dominant Sea of Marmara region.

By the 1960s it was clear that Central Anatolia was developing sufficiently to be considered part of Turkey's extended core regions, home to a dynamic and growing population in its own right. Put simply, the core regions that the Turks are primarily concerned with are now 300 kilometers (about 180 miles) closer to the Caucasus than they were a century ago. As the line of what was considered Turkified and modernized crept ever eastward, the Turks found themselves encroaching upon the largest remaining Anatolian minority: the Kurds. Just as the need to secure the eastern frontier for military reasons during World War I resulted in conflict with the Armenians, the need to secure the eastern frontier for economic and cultural reasons during the Cold War led to two decades of Kurdish insurgency in the 1980s and 1990s.

This process is not over, although it is far from the only issue garnering the Turks' attention. While Russian power is hardly gone, its reach and strength pales in comparison to Soviet power. Soviet influence has largely been excised from Turkey's southern and northwestern flanks. Rather than being Soviet client states, Iraq is an American protectorate, Egypt an American ally and Syria an Iranian ally. NATO and the European Union have expanded to absorb all of the former Soviet satellite states of Central Europe, moving the Russian line of influence back from Eastern Thrace to the Carpathian Mountains. There is no power directly abutting contemporary Turkey's northern, western or southern borders with either the capacity or will to clash with the Turks. The modern state may not have the relative might of the Ottoman Empire, but the Turks' borders are more secure than they have been in centuries.

After nearly a century of neutrality or hunkering under a NATO-forged shield, the combination of the Soviet collapse and the internal consolidation of Turkish politics under the now-ruling Justice and Development Party has allowed Turkey the possibility of re-emerging as a major power on the world stage. But having security is not the same as having lavish opportunities. The NATO/EU presence in the Balkans prevents a return of Turkish power to the region nearly as effectively as it blocks a return of Russian power. There is ample room for a neo-imperial expansion into the Arab world, but the potential benefits are as thin as the potential costs are thick, as Turkey well knows from its own imperial past: The Ottomans went northwest into the Danube Basin for wealth and glory; they went into the Arab world only when they met overwhelming resistance in Europe.

The result is a Turkey that is sampling many options but not committing to any. Some of these experiments have turned out very badly for Turkey. In late 2009 and early 2010 Turkish officials attempted to heal relations with the post-Soviet state of Armenia. However, Turkish foreign policy and strategic thinking has been in a deep freeze for the past 90 years, and it was wholly unprepared for the realities of power politics in the Caucasus. In the aftermath of the Soviet collapse, Armenia has become a satellite state of the Russian Federation, and so Ankara's negotiations with Yerevan were, in reality, with Moscow. Russia deftly used Turkey's uninformed — and ultimately failed — efforts at peace with Armenia to damage greatly Ankara's standing with the other Caucasus states, particularly Azerbaijan. In doing so, Russia improved its position in the Caucasus from the leading power in the region to the predominant.

Similarly, when Turkish organizations attempted to break through the Israeli blockade around the Gaza Strip in May 2010, Ankara mistakenly saw the opportunity for a public relations coup that would endear Turkey to the various states of the Middle East. While Turkey's anti-Israeli stance may have garnered it goodwill from the Arab street, it came at a very high cost. Instead of building gravitas with the Arab states, Ankara earned their rage as none of the Arab governments have an interest in an independent Palestinian entity. And of course the Turkish handling of the incident deeply damaged interests with Turkey's longtime ally, Israel.

This lack of an obvious path for any renewed Turkish expansion, combined with a relative lack of recent experience in influencing its own near abroad, actually makes it easier to predict Turkish actions for the next few years. Turkey will not be setting the agenda for the region, but instead reacting to the efforts of others. Before we can explore what those reactions will be, we must first examine the positions of the other major powers in the region.

CHAPTER 4:
Iran's Preventative Strategy

As the only successful mountain country, Iran has unique constraints and opportunities in dealing with the rest of the world.

Somewhat ironically, the most notable benefit is the difficulty of moving goods and people from place to place. Economies of scale rarely occur in mountain countries. As there are no navigable rivers that can help with shipping, most pieces of infrastructure do not build upon others, and much of the infrastructure required traverses economically useless regions simply to link any useful areas together. While this condemns mountain states to be crushingly poor — and Iran is no exception to that rule — it also makes invading mountain states a painful and expensive experience.

Invading a mountain state often requires building infrastructure to facilitate the movement of forces, followed by a massive occupation effort that must place soldiers in each and every mountain valley. As American forces have discovered in Afghanistan, even attempting to engage an entire region simultaneously is impossible without the advantage of sheer numbers, and changing such an area to something more to the occupiers' liking is only possible so long as the occupation is perpetual. Also, the same economic disadvantages that plague the natives bedevil any occupier, largely eliminating any possible economic advantages of occupation. Because of this, Persia has existed — despite its poverty — in some form for nearly the entirety of recorded human history.

Put simply, Persia/Iran is a permanent fixture of the region and, as such, its strengths and weaknesses require a closer examination than the other two major powers, which have "only" participated in Caucasus affairs for a few centuries. Again, Persia's mountainous nature guides our understanding.

Mountains are also known for fickle weather, so their peoples must cope with irregular cycles of feast and famine. The result is chronic social and even demographic instability, including periods of vast over- and under-population. In the pre-modern era, this led Persia into periods of vast expansion as it simply threw its excess population into imperial extension efforts — not so much not caring if the excess population ever returned but actually hoping that it would not. At present, Iran is in a state of a relative demographic dearth. Birth rates collapsed precipitously in the 1990s. This hardly means that Iran now has an insular foreign policy, but it does mean that Iran does not have a mass excess of population of war-fighting age, and even more notably there is no glut of those somewhat younger who would replace any who die. This somewhat constrains its military options for affecting its immediate neighborhood.

Just as in the Caucasus, in Iran there are different identities in every mountain valley, and it is very rare for the people in one valley to have any contact with peoples four or more valleys over. Holding a mountain state together is incredibly difficult. The four strategies the Persians have used to manage the heterogeneous nature of their population greatly enhance their ability to influence their near abroad.

First, Persia has embarked upon a timeless effort to expand its cultural reach, most notably within its own borders. By offering limited opportunities for non-Persian ethnics to participate in Persian society, broadly approving of intermarriage when it occurs and at times even redefining "Persian" as a cultural rather than ethnic term, the Persian nation has steadily extended "membership" to non-Persian ethnics inhabiting the Elburz and Zagros mountains. This has ever-so-slowly shifted the demographic balance in favor of the Persians. It is a work in progress: as of 2011, only 51 percent of Iranian citizens define themselves as ethnically Persian.

Second, contemporary Tehran has used modern Iran's oil wealth to maintain a subsidy system that can limit social pressures. Food, gasoline, electricity and housing are all items heavily subsidized for the majority of the Persian population. As of 2010, the collective bill for those subsidies came to about $100 billion, or one-third of contemporary Iran's gross domestic product (GDP).

Third, to prevent the constellation of minorities from rising up against the dominant Persians, in many ways Iran occupies itself. The country has always maintained an extremely large, infantry-heavy force, stationing troops in large numbers throughout its territory — even within its core. While this force obviously serves a defensive/deterrent purpose, its primary purpose is to ensure that the various ethnicities within Persian territories do not challenge Persian supremacy. Tehran does not shy away from using physical force against those who would challenge the Persian system, as the quick and brutal suppression of the 2010 Green Revolution demonstrated.

Fourth, to ensure loyalty of the general population, the Persians augment their military with one of the world's largest intelligence networks. Iranian society can be characterized by steadily rising tensions that lead to a brutal crackdown by the omnipresent military; Iranian intelligence serves a tripwire function for this, notifying the military when to act. The intelligence apparatus thus works better when there is an obvious military component, which can be hard to come by in places not already occupied by the Iranian military, much less in areas actively hostile to Iran.

Iran's intelligence capabilities contrast starkly with those of its most direct competitor in the Caucasus: Russia. Moscow historically has permanently stationed large standing military forces on its borders, leaving responsibility for domestic control to Russia's intelligence apparatus. This apparatus is accustomed to working without military cover, and so is more effective at eliciting cooperation in areas not formally under Russian control — such as the contemporary Caucasus — and better at maintaining relationships once they are established without regular military recourse.

This hardly means Iranian intelligence is incompetent; indeed, it is among the world's best. This is rather to say that Russia's intelligence services are far superior at manipulating populations when they cannot benefit from the direct presence of their military, which is typically the case when operating beyond national borders. The past 10 years offer many examples of places where Russian and Iranian intelligence have dueled for influence — Azerbaijan, Armenia, Turkmenistan and Tajikistan — and the Russians have prevailed in all competitions.

Despite this relative disadvantage, Iran clearly is the power that has the best long-term chances of influencing the Caucasus region. Perhaps most important is the simple factor of proximity. Turkey must cross some 700 kilometers (about 450 miles) of the rugged Anatolian plateau, a region that even after decades of development still has thin infrastructure. The Russian core is more than four times as far from the intra-Caucasus region than the Persian core is, but in practical terms the Russians are even further away. There is a bubble of nearly unpopulated arid lands to the northwest of the Caspian Sea. To reach the Caucasus, Russian power must follow more populated regions with infrastructure that instead arc to the southwest into Ukraine, before crossing the Don and arching back to the southeast along the coast of the Black Sea to the Caucasus. All told, this route is some 2,500 kilometers. In contrast, the Persian core territories in the Elburz and Zagros Mountains lie directly adjacent to the South Caucasus; contemporary Azerbaijan is particularly exposed.

Then there is the issue of standing forces. While Iran's manpower-heavy military is not expeditionary, it is large and omnipresent, and its permanent deployment means that Iran can surge forces without a mobilization. These characteristics allow Iran to seize strategic — perhaps even tactical — surprise, and choose the time and place of military conflict. Considering the smallish size of the populations of Azerbaijan and Georgia compared to Iran, that translates very quickly into Persian subjugation of the Caucasus unless another major power becomes involved.

Finally, there is the simple issue of need. Persia is a cocktail of ethnicities, and two of those ethnicities — the Kurds and ethnic Azerbaijanis — also exist in large numbers beyond the borders of contemporary Iran. The Kurds are not a significant threat; they lack a state, and the bulk of their population is in Turkey, a state that frowns upon any sort of Kurdish independence-minded activity. The ethnic Azerbaijanis, however, are a problem for Iran. There are more ethnic Azerbaijanis in Iran (12-18 million) than there are in independent Azerbaijan (8 million out of a total population of 9 million). Additionally, the Azerbaijanis of Azerbaijan are in the midst of a long-term military buildup in preparation for what they see as a necessary war to reclaim Nagorno-Karabakh. Tehran would much rather see Azerbaijan consumed with internal issues than developing a modern military designed to reclaim mountainous territory lost to the Armenians, because in the Persian mind there is not a great deal of difference between "liberating" Nagorno-Karabakh for the greater good of Azerbaijan and "liberating" Iranian Azerbaijan for the same purpose.

But just because Persia can easily dominate the Caucasus does not mean that it must do so, now or ever.

While Azerbaijan's growing military does ring alarm bells, Iran does not fear that Azerbaijan — or any native Caucasus power — could overthrow the Iranian government. In any incarnation Caucasus states simply lack the population necessary to launch a sustained, large-scale invasion of the Zagros/Elburz regions. Neither is the Caucasus en route to a region that it might be in Tehran's strategic interest to conquer. To the north lies the vastness of the Eurasian steppe, while Persia could approach the Levant and Marmara without first moving through the Caucasus. As far as usefulness in both forestalling an attack and being the first step to forming an imperium, Mesopotamia is a far more likely target of Persian attention than the Caucasus. Only on rare occasions have the Persians ever ventured past the Lesser Caucasus, much less the Greater Caucasus.

The most important reason for not conquering the intra-Caucasus region, however, is Iran's desire to limit exposure. Iran lacks a permanent reason to ever venture out of its mountain fastness. Its force structure is built for mountainous occupation, so moving into the flatlands of the intra-Caucasus region (or Central Asia or Mesopotamia) undermines many of Iran's strategic defenses. The largest concern

21

would be clashing with another major power more accustomed to operating on flat terrain in flat terrain. Russia has traditionally played that role, and on the four occasions since 1700 that Persia has crept northward it has clashed with — and lost to — the Russians. Entering the intra-Caucasus region provides very few advantages for Iran at a very high cost. This makes dealing with Azerbaijan particularly niggling. While Iran could quite easily overwhelm its northern neighbor, doing so would invite exactly the sort of broader conflict that Tehran does not want.

In these circumstances, Iran's attitude toward the Caucasus follows three guiding principles. First, secure the border as far north as possible while remaining secure in the mountains. The current border is probably in about as positive a position as it can be for Persian interests: anchored in the Elburz Mountains, where rainfall is higher, leaving the arid plains of Azerbaijan for others.

Second, ensure that the region remains as ethnically complex as possible to frustrate the ability of any other power to dominate the region. Iran will support any group in the region against any other stronger force in order to maintain the region's heterogeneity. In recent years this has translated into (often indirect) support for Armenia against Azerbaijan, despite the fact that both Azerbaijan and Iran are majority Shia, and Kurds against either Iraq or Turkey, despite the risk that supporting Kurdish separatism could entice Iran's own Kurdish minority to action.

Third, prevent, forestall or otherwise complicate the formation of a coherent military threat in the eastern Caucasus lowlands directly abutting the Persian core. In this, Iran faces more complications. A powerful Azerbaijan with a potent military that can reconquer Nagorno-Karabakh (and perhaps defeat Armenia) is the second-to-last thing Tehran wants to transpire in the Caucasus.

But the last thing Iran would want is for Russia to see its Armenian proxy threatened and to launch the sort of military operation against Azerbaijan that it did against Georgia in 2008, complete with additional Russian forces in Armenia and perhaps even some in Azerbaijan. Iran is against an independent Azerbaijan, but the likely outcomes of current Azerbaijani policies truly frighten Tehran. To that end, the Iranians are steadily deepening their intelligence penetration into Azerbaijan in order to force Baku to deal with internal issues, with the hopes of preventing Baku from progressing too far down the road to military competence — and igniting what Iran would see as a regional conflagration hostile to its interests regardless of the outcome.

CHAPTER 5:
Russia's Unique Position

Russia faces a very different set of security concerns from Turkey or Iran. Turkey has the benefits of peninsulas, water and mountains to shield it from enemies, while the trade opportunities of the Sea of Marmara ensure that even in lean times it has a steady income stream to help gird its natural defenses. Iran is made of mountains, and any attacker that seeks battle with it faces a daunting challenge under any circumstances. Iran may always be poor, but it is nearly always secure.

Russia, in contrast, is the very epitome of insecurity. The Russian core region of Muscovy sits on the Northern European Plain, and within 2,000 kilometers (about 1,200 miles) in any direction there are no appreciable natural defensive bulwarks. The only way in which a Russian entity can achieve some degree of security is to conquer its neighbors and use them as buffers. However, since Muscovy's immediate neighbors also lack natural geographic barriers, the expand-and-buffer strategy must be repeated until Russia's frontiers meet a physical barrier. The Greater Caucasus chain is one such barrier.

Such a security strategy has four implications for Russia's interaction with the region.

First, the expand-and-buffer strategy requires a massive, forward-deployed, low-tech army. The Russian strategy of security through expansion burdens Russia with larger territories and longer borders to defend, and because of the sheer distances involved, repeatedly repositioning small, highly mobile forces is not an option. Large, static forces must be maintained on all vulnerable borders, which is to say nearly every border, at all times. The cost of such forces is burdensome in the best of times, and the more successful Russia's security strategy is, the higher its costs.

In these circumstances, economic strength is seen as a distant concern that is regularly subordinated to the omnipresent military needs of the state, so Russia does not rule its territories with an eye for economic expansion like the Turks do. And unlike Iran, which is poor because of its geography, Russia is poor because of its military doctrine. Poverty, therefore, is seen in Moscow as an unavoidable outcome to be tolerated rather than a shortcoming to be corrected. This general lack of interest in economic opportunities carries into the Caucasus as well. In the modern age, the Russians do not feel a strong need to dominate the Azerbaijani energy sector (so long as Azerbaijani wealth does not threaten Russia's broader interests), as economic tools are somewhat removed from centuries of Russian strategic doctrine.

Second, the expand-and-buffer strategy requires a robust intelligence apparatus. Forcibly absorbing multiple ethnicities — and then using them on the front lines — does not make one particularly popular with those populations. However, because of Russia's large and often-expanding territory, Moscow cannot militarily occupy these populations as the Persians do — the military is needed on the frontier. Consequently, Russia has been forced to develop a robust internal intelligence capacity to patrol these populations and prevent them from breaking away. Since Russia's geography forces this security strategy, this intelligence apparatus has been a part of the Russian system for as long as there has been a Russian system — more to the point, it is normally fused with the political system. As such, the apparatus is the most-used tool in foreign policy, particularly in regions like the Caucasus, where there are many players and few concrete relationships.

Third, Russia sees its position on the northern slopes of Greater Caucasus as utterly non-negotiable. Of the various physical barriers that Russia can reach in its expansion, the Greater Caucasus is by far the closest to being airtight. The Carpathians have several passes and only shield Russia against the Balkans — Northern Europe has direct access via the Northern European Plain. Russia can anchor in the Tien Shen Mountains south of Central Asia, but this requires projecting power across a series of extremely arid regions, and like the Carpathians, the Tien Shen are not a perfect barrier, nor do they block all Asiatic access, as the Mongol invasion proved. But the Greater Caucasus have very few passes — all of which are closed in the winter — and the two coastal approaches around the Greater Caucasus chain are narrow and easily defended in comparison to the Northern European Plain or Eurasian steppe. Should Russia begin to degrade because of demographic decline, economic catastrophe or any other mix of maladies, retreating from the northern slopes of the Greater Caucasus will be among the last things Russia would do before dying, because the cost-benefit ratio of security gains from being there is so favorable.

Fourth, while Russia's instinct is to expand, the cost-benefit ratio inverts once it moves south of the ridge of the Greater Caucasus range. The most obvious reason is distance. The intra-Caucasus region is well removed from the Russian core. Climate and topography has resulted in a crescent-shaped population pattern that arcs west from the Northern Caucasus to Ukraine before arcing back northeast to the Russian core at Moscow. Because of this twist of climatic and demographic geography, the intra-Caucasus region is actually considerably further from Moscow than the flight line of 1,600 kilometers suggests — not to mention that the region is on the opposite side of Moscow's best geographic barrier.

There are also two nearby competing major powers — Turkey and Iran — in the intra-Caucasus region, and both of these powers' relations with the Russians historically have been cool at best. The intra-Caucasus region also has a local population, the Georgians, with a very strong national identity. The Georgians are also numerous — had Georgia remained in the Russian Federation at the time of the Soviet breakup, Georgians would have become Russia's largest minority group. Taken together, Russia has few pressing needs — and faces many pressing complications — when it ventures south of the Greater Caucasus.

Unlike Turkey, Russia's view of the Caucasus has not markedly changed in the past two centuries. The region has been the greatest southern extension of Russian power, with Russian influence first reaching it in the 18th century. The czars fought a series of bloody occupation campaigns to pacify the various Turkic ethnicities of the northern slopes of the Greater Caucasus, a process which often overlapped with a constant barrage of Russo-Ottoman and Russo-Persian wars of the 18th and 19th centuries. Nevertheless, it was not until the end of World War I that the region was pulled fully into the Russian orbit. For the first time in centuries, the Caucasus ceased to be a field of competition among the three major regional powers and instead was transformed into a wholly internal territory.

While first attempting to rule the entire intra-Caucasus region as a single entity, Russia united the region under the Transcaucasian Democratic Federal Republic and then the Transcaucasian Socialist Federative Soviet Republic. But after 14 years of infighting among the regions, Moscow concluded that a divide-and-conquer strategy would be easier. In 1936, the Union of Soviet Socialist Republics (USSR) was created, and Moscow split their Transcaucasian entity into three entities — as well as a series of enclaves to partially separate the fractious groups from each other. The modern incarnations of Armenia, Azerbaijan, Georgia, Nagorno-Karabakh, Nakhchivan, Abkhazia, South Ossetia and Adjara were born.

Throughout this period, internal uprisings were common, but unlike in previous periods the small nations of the region could not count on the support of either Persia or Turkey. Over the course of decades, all the uprisings were ground down. One particularly draconian — if effective — technique used to quell rebellions was the mass deportation of problematic groups to Siberia and the steppes of Central Asia. Chechens, Ingush, Balkars, Kurds, Meskhetian Turks and more were all relocated by the hundreds of thousands.

The result was a tense stability made possible by the overwhelming power and presence of the Soviet internal security apparatus. The Russians ruled the entire region as an internal territory, but that control shattered in 1991 with the disintegration of the Soviet Union.

CHAPTER 6:
The Russian Collapse

Soviet political leader Mikhail Gorbachev knew that the USSR was falling further behind the West economically, demographically and even militarily. His plan was to use perestroika and glasnost reforms to attract Western technology and managerial expertise to rejuvenate the Soviet system and save it from a slow-motion death. In the end, however, Gorbachev's plans led to the Soviet Union's demise.

In the years that followed the collapse, it was far from certain that Russian power would survive at all. The political elite of the Communist system was shattered and discredited, and the reformers initially backed by Gorbachev fell into disarray as well. Power was shared by two groups: the oligarchs, a new class of Russian businessmen who proceeded to strip the state of its most valuable assets; and the siloviki, a then-coalition of military and foreign ministry personnel who yearned for a return to the height of Soviet power. Neither group was as simple as this description suggests. Some oligarchs had generals in their pockets, some siloviki engaged in oligarchic practices, and others such as government bureaucrats, former intelligence officials and even members of the Cabinet regularly supplied assistance to one group or another. But the duality of the oligarch-siloviki split is a solid starting point for understanding 1990s Russian power balances. Between the two groups was the largely incompetent government of the easily manipulated Boris Yeltsin.

For the most part, the oligarchs had no interest in actually ruling Russia; they simply wanted to use the state as a vehicle for transferring Russian state wealth to themselves. The siloviki may have wanted to improve governance, but they had no expertise in doing so; the intelligence apparatus, not the military, had managed the Soviet system. The intelligence factions did not began to re-enter the equation until the late 1990s and early 2000s. What passed as government until then was in essence a tug-of-war between the early siloviki and oligarchs who lacked either the desire or the ability to rehabilitate the state.

The result was a multi-year economic, political, social and military freefall culminating in the August 1998 ruble crisis, which simultaneously destroyed what was left of the Soviet fabric and ironically set the stage for the return of key portions of the Soviet system.

Mikhail Gorbachev's efforts of perestroika and glasnost had a host of different effects across the USSR, but in the Caucasus, the efforts led directly to chaos. Russian power throughout the region was based on deep intelligence penetration and control combined with a very large, forward-stationed military presence on the Soviet border with Turkey and Iran. When that presence became less overbearing, the tense, artificially imposed stability of the region quickly began to break down.

Well before the Soviet Union was formally dissolved in December 1991, unrest was erupting in the Caucasus. Armenia and Azerbaijan started launching pogroms against each other's co-ethnics as early as late 1987. Ingush-Ossetian racial conflicts, which boiled into war in 1992, first turned deadly in 1988. Abkhaz-Georgian race riots began in Georgia in July 1989. The two Georgian enclaves of Abkhazia and South Ossetia formally declared independence in August 1990. Chechnya declared — and exercised — independence in January 1991. And Armenia and Azerbaijan were engaged in full warfare with each other over Nagorno-Karabakh months before the Soviet Union's official dissolution.

The Northern Caucasus

By the end of 1991, Russian power had been excised from south of the Greater Caucasus, and saying that Russian power remained in the Northern Caucasus between 1992 and 1999 is being somewhat charitable to the Russians.

Chechen independence epitomized the Russian problem. Moscow's physical security requires anchoring Russia's borders at certain geographic barriers, of which the Greater Caucasus are the most significant. The independence of Chechnya, lying on the northern slope of the mountain range, meant that anchor point was lost. And with the exception of the River Don there are no significant barriers lying between Chechnya and the Russian heartland.

In 1994, Russia responded to the Chechens' declaration of independence the only way it could: with an intervention meant to reclaim the territory and intimidate any other republics with separatist thoughts into docility. The war quickly turned into a two-year-long disaster that demonstrated just how far Russia's power had degraded. Russian columns destined for the Chechen capital of Grozny were regularly ambushed — and often outright destroyed. Russia could not even effectively patrol Chechnya's borders, with major Chechen military thrusts regularly pushing deep into adjacent republics.

The 1996 armistice was a massive embarrassment to the Kremlin and Russian military and had a demoralizing effect on the Russian psyche. It was obvious at the time that Russia was far too broken and chaotic in its core lands to be able to fight an actual war more than 2,000 kilometers (about 1,200 miles) from Moscow and in a fiercely difficult region. The best Russia could do at the time was to freeze the conflict, allowing Moscow to recover and get its house in order; however, the armistice also allowed the Chechen separatists to regroup, recruit and rearm for the next round of fighting.

Two other critical issues came out of the war. First was the spillover of the Russian-Chechen conflict into neighboring republics — particularly Dagestan, where Chechen fighters continually used the population as hostages, shields and recruits. This created a great deal of resentment between the Dagestani and Chechen populations, something that would spark the Second Chechen War in 1999.

The second issue was the entrance of the Chechens into the global jihadist network. The Russians had always charged that international

Muslim militants were involved in the First Chechen War, but there is no doubt that in the interwar period Chechens regularly traveled to Afghanistan for training and Arab militants began showing up in Chechnya and Dagestan en masse. The result was a religious radicalization of much of the Chechen, Ingush and Dagestani population that continues to intensify.

Overall, Russia's failure in the First Chechen War was a clear indicator of just how far it had fallen from its former status as a global power. The Russian people saw their military smashed in the Chechen war; their economy spiral into the abyss — businesses overtaken by foreigners, oligarchs and crooks; and a government stagger under a feeble leader. In short, the country had tumbled into chaos. Russia would need two things to get back on its feet: a leader with an iron fist and time to regroup. That would not happen until 1999.

The Intra-Caucasus

The peoples south of the Caucasus region hardly escaped the destruction of the Soviet Union unscathed. The three Soviet republics of the intra-Caucasus region — Armenia, Azerbaijan and Georgia — became independent countries, each with its own internal territorial issues.

The most drastic impact of the Soviet collapse was the near complete removal of the Soviet intelligence apparatus from the region. While that apparatus was undeniably responsible for the oppression of the region's various ethnicities and religions, it suppressed the often-violent interaction of those same ethnicities and religions. The sudden absence of that controlling factor led to an eruption of conflicts that, while stunning in their vitriol and number to outside observers, was seen by the local populations as an expected escalation.

But the unraveling of the Soviet system resulted in much more than "simply" internecine warfare. The presence of Soviet military equipment stores — the Caucasus was a border region and so had hosted a large, forward-stationed military force — allowed those conflicts to burn with an intensity unprecedented in the region's already

NET MIGRATION SINCE 1990

COUNTRY	MIGRATION	CURRENT POPULATION
Armenia	-915,000	3,262,200
Azerbaijan	-405,000	9,047,000
Georgia	-1,545,000	4,636,300

Source: United Nations Population Division

complicated and bloody history. Furthermore, the entire region faced complete economic collapse as the Soviet/Russian economy first severed its connections to the region and then collapsed in its own right.

Unprecedented population movements occurred. Largely due to the economic collapse, some 30 percent of the Armenian and Georgian populations and 10 percent of the Azerbaijani population left their home countries in search of work elsewhere. More than 1 million Armenians and Azerbaijanis were uprooted and relocated as the two states fell into war. Georgia faced separatist conflicts and eventual wars in South Ossetia and Abkhazia, both of which generated their own refugee flows. Planned population-swap programs resettled some nationalities who found themselves living on the wrong side of new national borders which had until recently been internal administrative divisions. As many as 100,000 Chechens returned to the Northern Caucasus from their Siberian and Kazakh exile. Thousands — perhaps tens of thousands — of Mesheti Turks returned to Georgia. With each movement, hostility built between the displaced, those who found themselves with new neighbors, and the old and new governing bodies of both groups.

Adapting to the post-Soviet economic realities would have been trying for any of the three states, but doing so against a backdrop of wars, mass refugee movements, mass emigration and mass exile returns stretched all three past the breaking point. Georgia arguably suffered the most and did not reassert control over most of its territory until 2007, and it has yet to reclaim its separatist regions of Abkhazia and South Ossetia.

Russia's absence from the Caucasus left it open to whomever wanted to expend the resources on expanding influence into the region. However, neither Turkey nor Iran were in a position to take advantage of the Soviet collapse. Turkey's re-emergence as a power was not yet under way. In Turkey, the 1990s were a time of insurgency, political instability and internal consolidation. In Iran, the issue of the day was recovering from a crushing, eight-year war with Iraq while watching U.S. military actions against Iraq with a mix of hope and dread. Moreover, both powers were so accustomed to the KGB's iron wall in the Caucasus that they were hesitant to attempt any push in that direction. In this, both powers missed their window of opportunity to take hold of the Caucasus before Russia regrouped and moved back in. This allowed only one power — from the other side of the world — a chance to shape the region: the United States.

CHAPTER 7:
The American Moment and the Caucasus Economy

Throughout the 1990s, the Caucasus region suffered from the undoing of what economic development occurred during the Soviet era. With the exception of Azerbaijan's newly built energy industry, is little economic activity anywhere in the region.

The region boasts no navigable rivers, and thus no supplies of local capital. Georgia has two decent anchorages on its Black Sea coast, but they are in regions populated by rebellious minorities. Were the intra-Caucasus states combined into a single body, they might achieve some economies of scale, but as separate entities, they not only compete for scarce resources but also must use those resources to defend against each other.

The region also cannot serve as an extension of a nearby economy, simply because there is not an economy nearby that is interested. The closest economic hub by far is the Sea of Marmara region — the nerve center of modern Turkey (and previously, the Ottoman Empire and Byzantium). But not only is the intra-Caucasus region some 1,000 kilometers (about 600 miles) away, the far richer eastern Balkans are much closer and serviced by a navigable waterway. Even if the development capital and modes of transport somehow were to become available in the Caucasus, anything produced in the region would still face transport costs so onerous that they would negate any economic usefulness the region might otherwise boast.

As such, Armenia, Azerbaijan and Georgia did not experience their first real industrialization until the Soviet period, and that process was designed to lash the three to Moscow more than to create any sort of functional economic structures. Successful development required industrial plants designed, built, maintained and paid for by Russians, and, perhaps most importantly, nearly all of these industries were only functional as part of the greater whole of the Soviet system. When that system collapsed, the skilled labor, capital and operating technology all left. Such a holistic design meant that even had the Caucasus peoples had the money and skills necessary to operate the industries, they still would not have had access to the other portions of the supply chain required to make their newly independent economies functional.

The scale of new investment required to repurpose the Soviet-era industry simply does not exist within the Caucasus states, as two examples elsewhere in the post-Soviet world vividly demonstrate: Russia itself and East Germany.

Throughout the 1990s, Russia attempted to wrestle its Soviet-era industry into a new form more amenable to the post-Cold War world. Being the core of the old Soviet Union, the new Russian Federation contained the vast majority of the Soviet population, infrastructure and industrial base, so Russia's relative adjustment was the smallest out of all of the former Soviet states. After 15 years, some industries were indeed retooled to keep operating. However, shorn of captive markets and now chronically exposed to the option of cheaper and higher-quality imports from the West and East Asia, most of these industries were simply — if belatedly — shuttered. Russia today has retained an industrial base, but it is mostly geared toward the production of primary commodities (such as oil, natural gas, timber, wheat, diamonds and palladium) and secondary commodities (such as aluminum, steel and lumber). The former Soviet/Russian consumer and manufacturing industries are almost completely gone.

East Germany, which at independence had a population similar to that of the three Caucasus states combined, represented the most advanced industrial base in the Soviet sphere, populated by the highest-skilled workers in the Soviet sphere. Upon the end of the USSR's satellite system and the inclusion of East Germany into the Federal

Republic of Germany, Berlin and Bonn worked to upgrade the old Soviet-era industry to Western standards and integrate it into West Germany's supply chains. After 10 years and $1 trillion — backed up by massive skilled labor transfers, subsidizations and income support not part of the refurbishment funds — the decision was made to simply scrap most of the Soviet-era industrial base en masse. More than a decade after that decision was made, East Germany is only now beginning to contribute again to the broader German economy. It will likely be two generations before the German economy can truly be considered a single system.

If the German political commitment to reunification backed by Germany's economic strength cannot rehabilitate Soviet-era industry, it is difficult to imagine how any confluence of forces — particularly local Caucasus forces — could generate a better result. Any such efforts face the additional challenge of many regional powers having an interest in keeping some or all portions of the Caucasus' economies from succeeding.

Consequently, the sharp contraction in economic activity caused by the Soviet collapse should not be viewed as something that is reversible with a combination of patience and outside assistance. Unless those industries can be easily redirected toward foreign markets, they are gone and will not return. Industries that could be repurposed are those that have since powered the Russian resurgence: oil, natural gas, ores, metals and other primary and secondary commodities, and even these industries can only be saved if the raw materials they require are present locally. At that time, much of Ukraine's steel industry withered when Russian iron ore became hard to come by, just as several Central Asian oil refineries are now largely shuttered because oil that Soviet central planning once made available now flows elsewhere.

Not much is left of Caucasus industry. Armenia and Georgia import nearly all the goods they consume, including most of their foodstuffs and all of their oil and natural gas. The two export little other than a smattering of ores, agricultural exports and scrap metals. Each has a trade deficit of about 30 percent of GDP, a burden that can only be sustained by direct subsidization from Russia (in

CAUCASUS STATES' AGRICULTURAL AND FOOD SUPPLY BALANCE

COMMODITY	NET IMPORTS (MILLION TONS)	IMPORTS AS A % OF TOTAL CONSUMPTION
GEORGIA		
Wheat	650	87%
Sugar	100	100%
Corn	50	20%
Edible oil	70	75%
Barley	5	24%
ARMENIA		
Wheat	275	54%
Sugar	82	96%
Rice	5	100%
AZERBAIJAN		
Wheat	1,225	41%
Sugar	165	89%
Corn	75	33%
Rice	10	100%

Sources: United States Department of Agriculture, and Food and Agriculture Organization of the United Nations

Armenia's case) and indirect subsidization from the United States via the International Monetary Fund (IMF) and World Bank (in Georgia's case). As of 2010, both countries count external transfers — whether from massive populations who have left in search of work or charity payments from the Armenian diaspora — as their primary

TOP TRADING PARTNERS

COUNTRY	VALUE*	% OF TOTAL TRADE	% OF GDP
GEORGIA			
Turkey	1104.7	16.5%	9.44%
Azerbaijan	708.1	10.6%	6.05%
Ukraine	662.2	9.9%	5.66%
Germany	361.8	5.4%	3.09%
China	358.6	5.4%	3.06%
ARMENIA			
Russia	995.1	20.8%	10.59%
China	463.7	9.7%	4.93%
Germany	346.3	7.2%	3.68%
Iran	269.7	5.6%	2.87%
Bulgaria	269.0	5.6%	2.86%
AZERBAIJAN			
Italy	7198.2	25.8%	13.90%
France	1980.9	7.0%	3.82%
Russia	1925.1	7.0%	3.72%

*In million USD
Sources: EIU Country Report

source of income. For Armenia, diaspora support equals one-fifth of GDP.

The Caucasus' various microcommunities, such as the separatist Nagorno-Karabakh and Abkhazia, are in even worse economic shape. They are far smaller and more rugged than Armenia or Georgia, so all the concerns about a lack of local capital, markets and economies of scale are magnified. The Russian proxies of Abkhazia and South Ossetia are particularly dependent upon Russian largess for all their energy consumption, nearly all their food and nearly all their military budgets. What passes as an economy in these regions consists of little more than smuggling goods across the borders (although Abkhazia does boast a bona fide tourist industry, though even this is a fraction of what it was during Soviet times).

Luckily for Azerbaijan, some of these trends do not apply to it. The extensive irrigation systems developed under Soviet rule still function, lessening the need for food imports (Azerbaijan imports only about 40 percent of its wheat). Soviet-era energy infrastructure enabled Azerbaijan to be oil self-sufficient upon independence. In recent years, Azerbaijan's energy sector has increased in output by more than an order of magnitude, but to understand this dramatic evolution we must first examine the role of the power that made Azerbaijan's energy industry possible.

The United States

Normally, STRATFOR begins discussions of cross-regional strategic issues with the position of the United States because the United States is the only country in the world that can project power — whether economic, political or military — anywhere on the planet. This discussion did not start in this manner, however, because currently the United States does not have a large stake in the Caucasus. It is not that Russia, Iran and Turkey are sufficiently powerful to prevent American influence from penetrating — although that is indeed the case — as much as the Americans are preoccupied with other portions of the world.

Since the 9/11 attacks, the Americans have been distracted with events in the Islamic world, focusing most of their deployable military units and foreign policy capabilities there. Ten years after the attacks, the Americans are only now beginning to unwind those efforts, and it will be years before they have the degree of military and political flexibility they possessed before the attacks. Until that happens, it is difficult to see the United States taking a firm stance in any region as remote and difficult as the Caucasus.

Such was not always the case. As the Soviet Union collapsed, it took down its entire network of client and satellite states with it. Foreign powers wasted little time surging influence into every nook and cranny of the old Soviet empire. The Europeans, haltingly at first, moved into the former Soviet satellite states of Central Europe: All of those states are now both NATO and EU members, and while Russian influence does still exist, it is far weaker than Moscow's Cold war-era iron grip. Turkey experimented with a similar influence surge into Central Asia. China did the same into Mongolia and Southeast Asia. And every power with the capability moved into Africa and the Middle East.

What set the United States apart from all of the others is that it was present in every region and often was the most powerful external player in each one. Nothing epitomizes the extreme change in power balances of the 1990s better than the U.S. penetration into the Caucasus.

The Caucasus stands out among the regions the Americans reached for in the 1990s because there was no overriding reason for the U.S. effort. A pro-American intra-Caucasus region would not have directly enhanced American security by any measurable amount. Unlike U.S. efforts in Latin America, efforts in the Caucasus were not protecting Washington's backyard or pursuing trade opportunities. Unlike Central Europe, there was no Cold War insurance policy to cash in on in the Caucasus. Unlike East Asia, there were no navigation rights crucial to the projection of American power. Unlike Africa, resources were thin. Unlike the Middle East, even energy was not much of a lure, as any energy produced in the Caucasus flows to Southern European markets, not North America. But most importantly — and unlike any of the other regions — a sustained American presence in the Caucasus would have required a sustained, large-scale effort. Washington had no potential ally in the region of sufficient power to hold against Russia and/or Persia without significant, ongoing outside support.

Instead of economic gain, the U.S. entrance into the Caucasus served one purpose: an effort at reshaping destinies. Simply put, the Americans hoped that they could impose sufficient order upon the region so that its dominant power would be Washington's long-time ally, Turkey, rather than a Russia stumbling from the Cold War's end or an Iran still healing from the Iran-Iraq war.

In the Turks, the Americans originally had enthusiastic partners. Turkish insularity appeared to be waning with the end of the Cold War, and with the Russians and Iranians distracted, the perfect conditions for a new Turkish expansion seemed to have arisen. However, two developments delayed the Turkish revival. The Turkish politician most enamored of the Caucasus and Central Asia, President Turgut Ozal, died in April 1993, and his death contributed to the collapse of the government and a period of several years of government instability, culminating in a soft military coup in 1998. Turkey did not consolidate internally until the mid-2000s and only began searching for a framework for its new foreign policy in 2010. That framework is still being explored, and until it is formed, Turkish actions in the international system will lack sustainability and focus.

Without a partner whose desires and policies could shape — and maintain — the broader effort, American activity in the Caucasus became erratic in target, effort level and attention. In Azerbaijan and Georgia, the Americans actively supported the authoritarian governments of Heydar Aliyev and Eduard Shevardnadze, largely because their international stature as former Soviet Politburo members gave them the expertise and gravitas to wrestle their respective governments into some sort of shape. In Armenia, the Americans did not even try to keep up with the never-ending parade of changing leaders — Armenia had nine prime ministers in the decade after the Soviet collapse — and largely ignored that Armenia was a Russian satellite state. The Armenian diaspora in the United States proved able to manipulate Congress and the State Department to shower the country with more aid per capita than any entities save Israel and the Palestinian Authority. Rumors — never proven, but credible enough to be taken seriously — even indicated that American intelligence played all sides of the Chechen conflict in order to keep Russia off balance.

The Americans were attempting to use the region as a spring-board for the projection of Western influence into the lands north, south and east of the Caucasus as well as preclude any possibility of a Russian-Iranian alliance. Unfortunately for the American effort, the Caucasus is not naturally set up for such a purpose. The three minor states were hardly of one mind — after all, Armenia and Azerbaijan were in a state of de facto war during most of this period. Due to differences in ethnic and linguistic backgrounds, the intra-Caucasus states had little ability to influence lands beyond their immediate borders (and in many cases, even within their borders). The United States also had no historical connections to the region, so relations had to be built from scratch. The Americans also failed to understand that the Russians and Persians saw themselves as competitors rather than partners in the Caucasus (and, ironically, that a successful American effort to separate Russia and Iran would have limited their fields of competition and actually made a Russo-Persian alliance more likely).

Yet as inconsistent as American policy was in the region in the 1990s, the United States was still the world's most powerful country, and at the time, there simply was no meaningful external competition for the region's future. American power successfully rewired many of the relationships within the region, even if only for a few years. This built up an expectation in Armenia and Azerbaijan that there was a new player and convinced the Georgians that this new power could reinforce an independent Tbilisi. Yet once the Americans began their wars in the Islamic world, Washington's attention span in the Caucasus dwindled. The August 2008 Russo-Georgian war made abundantly clear that while the United States might still have influence in the region, its ability to set the Caucasus agenda had lapsed.

The United States did leave an imprint in the Caucasus, however, as it saw to completion the negotiation, financing and construction of Azerbaijan's modern energy industry. That industry transformed Azerbaijan from a remote, impoverished country into a major energy exporter, producing some 1 million barrels per day of crude oil and

AZERBAIJANI ENERGY

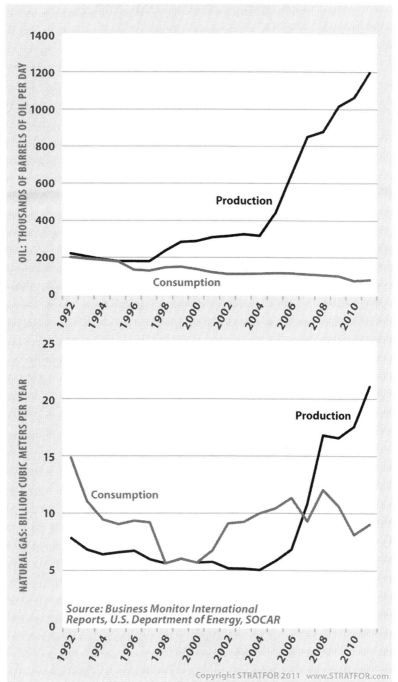

Source: Business Monitor International
Reports, U.S. Department of Energy, SOCAR

Copyright STRATFOR 2011   www.STRATFOR.com

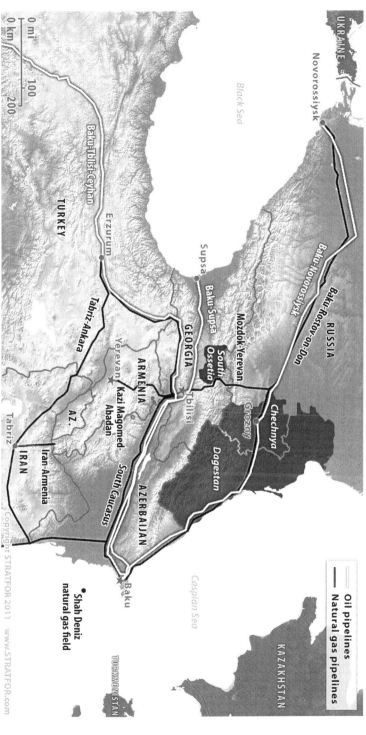

CAUCASUS ENERGY INFRASTRUCTURE

Oil pipelines
Natural gas pipelines

UKRAINE

Novorossiysk

Black Sea

Baku-Tbilisi-Ceyhan

TURKEY

Erzurum

Supsa

Baku-Supsa

Baku-Novorossiysk

Baku-Rostov-on-Don

RUSSIA

Mozdok-Yerevan

Tabriz-Ankara

GEORGIA

South Ossetia

Grozny

Chechnya

Yerevan

ARMENIA

Kazi Magomed-Abadan

Tbilisi

Dagestan

A.Z.

Tabriz

Iran-Armenia

IRAN

South Caucasus

AZERBAIJAN

Baku

Caspian Sea

Shah Deniz
natural gas field

TURKMENISTAN

KAZAKHSTAN

0 mi
0 km
100
200

Copyright STRATFOR 2011 www.STRATFOR.com

some 16 billion cubic meters of natural gas per year. The two key transport routes are known as the Baku-Tbilisi-Ceyhan oil pipeline and the South Caucasus natural gas pipeline. The energy corridor also broadly followed the original American plan, snaking through the intra-Caucasus region into Georgia and then southwest into Turkey, circumventing Russia. For the first time in history there was a robust economic reason to be in the intra-Caucasus region, and that moment had arrived just as the American moment had ended.

The largest implication of the American moment is that there is now a local Caucasus power — Azerbaijan — that has the economic wherewithal to achieve its goals, but lacks a committed sponsoring power to shape or moderate those goals. In the past, any local power in the Caucasus only rose to significance when all the major extra-Caucasus powers were weak or distracted. For the first time in the region's history, there is now a local power that could reshape the region to a limited degree while major powers are engaged. This unprecedented development will greatly shape intra-Caucasus developments for the next decade. (We will revisit this topic in Chapter 15.)

Despite its withdrawal, the United States is still a player in the region. Investments into regional energy developments alone mean that Washington will from time to time attempt to make its wishes a reality. And while largely removed from the region, the Americans still possess potent tools with a global reach — especially through the heavy subsidization of the IMF and World Bank in Georgia. Also, U.S. military aid grants Washington the ability to influence (and sometimes derail) the plans of Caucasus powers both large and small.

But the American absence — like the Soviet decline before it — has left the region open to whatever power has the need and is willing to invest the time and resources. As the United States lacks the ability to intervene militarily in the region, the real decisions that affect the Caucasus will be made in Ankara, Tehran and, most of all, a regenerated Moscow.

CHAPTER 8:
Russia Returns

From August 1998 through July 1999, Russia faced a chain of catastrophes. In August 1998, the financial crisis that had been plaguing East Asia for a year dealt Russia a double blow. The East Asian economic collapse had sent the prices of commodities — which accounted for 80 percent of Russian exports and most of the Russian government's income — through the floor. Stripped of funds, the Russian government defaulted on its debt, and the steady capital flight from the country increased strikingly. The stock markets and the ruble collapsed, and modern economic life halted. Concurrently, there were signs that a new Chechen War was about to break out. Chechen and jihadist Arab troops had been regularly sighted in the Northern Caucasus republic of Dagestan.

Russian power had collapsed abroad as well. Poland, the Czech Republic and Hungary, three former Soviet satellite states, joined NATO in March 1999. One of their first actions in NATO was to support an air assault campaign on the Russian client state of Yugoslavia (now Serbia) in March through June of that year. The Russians were humiliated and impoverished and had lost the ability to influence the world — indeed, even parts of their own country.

Against this backdrop, the power groups in Russia decided that to prevent a complete collapse, they needed a national leader somewhat stronger than the failing Boris Yeltsin. Shortly after one of Yeltsin's many heart attacks in the summer of 1999, representatives of the oligarchs and the siloviki met to select a new prime minister. Knowing that the oligarchs would reject a siloviki candidate and vice versa, they reached for a member of the country's third — and far smaller — power group: the St. Petersburg clan.

This clan was different from the other groups in two important ways. First, its power was largely limited to Baltic Russia, which historically has been more Europeanized and occasionally pro-Western in its mindset than Moscow — so neither the oligarchs nor the siloviki believed that the clan could possibly threaten their power centers in the rest of Russia. Second, and in part because their power was limited to a single region (and had been run as a de facto independent state for much of the 1990s), the St. Petersburg clan had an appreciation for all of the tools of state power, including economic management, intelligence oversight, military force and political manipulation.

The person the oligarchs and siloviki selected as their compromise proxy leader was Vladimir Putin. He was not a proxy leader for long. Putin's grounding in St. Petersburg, his intelligence background and his former espionage beat of stealing Western technology meant that he had allies in both the oligarch and siloviki camps.

Putin — who became prime minister in August 1999, acting president in January 2000, president-elect in March 2000 and president in May 2000 — wasted no time in reconsolidating central authority. In 2000, he instigated military reforms after the sinking of the Kursk submarine. By August 2001, he had partially consolidated both the oligarchs and the siloviki under his control, started breaking the back of a new Chechen rebellion in the Second Chechen War, balanced the budget, renegotiated (and paid down most of) Russia's international debts, empowered what was functionally a new single-party system and instilled Russians with a renewed sense of purpose and stability.

Putin's efforts were complemented by two developments largely beyond Russia's control. First, there was a strong global recovery in the demand for commodities. Prices rose smartly throughout 2000, and then again from 2002-2008. The income was more than enough for Moscow to stabilize the Russian economy, balance the national budget and have cash left over to fund a more aggressive foreign policy.

Second, the Americans' occasional intrusions into the former Soviet space ended in a roundabout way. After the 9/11 attacks, Putin also reached out to the United States, offering Russian intelligence and assistance in security bases in Central Asia to help Washington prosecute the war against al Qaeda, in the hopes of deflecting U.S. attention fully from the Russian sphere of influence. The strategy worked, but only after a fashion.

In the early 2000s, Washington successfully pushed for the admittance of the three Baltic states — all former Soviet republics — into NATO and indirectly supported a series of "color revolutions" across the former Soviet Union and started recruiting former Soviet states into NATO. The Kremlin became convinced that the Americans were trying to overturn Russian power. This had two implications. First, Russian cooperation with the Americans was greatly scaled back, with Russia steadily whittling away at U.S. access to Central Asia — access that was critical to fighting the war in Afghanistan. Second, the Putin government redoubled its efforts to consolidate its power in Russia and its near abroad to choke off foreign influence.

Then, in 2003, the United States invaded Iraq, and as time went on, the Americans' elation at the ease of their military victory in Baghdad gave way to a grim realization that it was only the opening scene of a multi-year occupation. The occupation, along with commitments in Afghanistan, effectively absorbed all of the United States' deployable ground combat troops and opened a window of opportunity for Russia to reconsolidate its hold on many of the former Soviet territories without American interference.

Part of Putin's rise and the Russian resurgence was the reinvigoration of the Russian intelligence services. Having one of their own at the top of the organizational pyramid was key to this recovery, and Putin quickly placed intelligence confidants in key positions throughout the Russian government and economy. By 2005, his intelligence allies held a majority of what was worth controlling, and by the time he completed his two presidential terms in 2008 the consolidation was, for all practical purposes, complete. Central control was so powerful that during the 2008 financial crisis — which was by most economic measures more harmful to Russia than even the 1998 ruble crash — there was hardly a ripple of public discontent toward the Kremlin. Instead, much of the population blamed the West for the crash, turning sentiment against Western economic models.

The Russian Resurgence in the Northern Caucasus

One of Putin's first major efforts upon rising to power was to tackle the Northern Caucasus problem once again. Chechen forces invaded Dagestan 17 days after Putin became prime minister, and he immediately committed the military. On Oct. 1, 1999, the Russian army began assaults in northern Chechnya. After four months of brutal fighting and thousands of casualties on both sides, the Russians had control of Grozny.

This is where Putin began changing Russian strategy, both for domestic and international reasons. Once the Chechen "state" had been broken, Russian forces faced dozens of armed groups that only loosely coordinated their efforts. Russian intelligence became instrumental in identifying these groups' leaders for elimination. In time, this shift toward intelligence in the war broke the back of the insurgency.

It was a long haul. The Russians did not formally declare victory in the Second Chechen War until April 2009. Nevertheless, while the conflict was a constant drag on the Russian system, it ironically proved to be the crucible in which the Putin government remade Russian power and prestige. The increased importance of intelligence in the war proved to be extremely popular. It sharply raised the profile of and respect for Putin's allies in the security services while diluting siloviki claims to be the true protectors of Russian sovereignty. In international relations, it also provided ample justification for a massive Russian military and intelligence presence in the Caucasus, which did far more than allow the Kremlin to reconsolidate its hold on the Northern Caucasus republics: It placed the tools it needed for reconsolidation of the intra-Caucasus region nearby.

Russian power on the northern slopes of the Greater Caucasus is essential for the existence of the Russian state. Militarily, there are no good geographic barriers where Russian forces can anchor themselves between the Greater Caucasus range and the Russian core territories. Anchoring in the Greater Caucasus, where the mountains can serve as a force multiplier, both grants Russia some security and slims Russia's defense cost; it no longer needs to station large, static forces throughout the lands north of the Greater Caucasus.

Yet as the Chechen situation stabilized, the Russians did not limit their presence in the region to north of the Greater Caucasus. Russia recently has ventured south of the Greater Caucasus range in force, and hardly because of habit or imperial nostalgia. It is a testament to the strength of Russian post-Cold War resurgence that it can play the Caucasus game to a much stronger degree than the two other regional players. In short, Russia is involved in the Greater Caucasus because it must be; when it gets involved in the intra-mountain region and the Lesser Caucasus, it is because it can be.

The Russian Resurgence in the Intra-Caucasus

Russia's first moves in the intra-Caucasus were varied and often less direct than anything Russia did in Chechnya. Russian intelligence assets were used to reshape political forces in entities that Russia does not directly control, to keep them as internally fractured as possible, with extra effort dedicated to states whose formal policies are anti-Russian. Georgia, in particular, was a target of this policy; Russian intelligence has proven remarkably adept at fracturing an already-disunited political elite. The same strategy was used with Azerbaijan, but it was applied with much less gusto, as Baku has adopted more favorable stance regarding Russian interests explicitly to avoid the sort of attention that Georgia habitually garners. This intelligence-penetration strategy has been successful in loosening Georgia's would-be alliance with the United States, preventing Georgia from unifying its own territory, driving a multitude of wedges between Azerbaijan and

Turkey and limiting Iran's ability to gain a foothold in either Armenia or Azerbaijan.

Russia's second tactic for reasserting itself in the Caucasus was economic. The intra-Caucasus states have little going for them economically, so throughout the 2000s the Russians selectively reconnected pieces of the old Soviet system to increase their tools for manipulation. Electricity lines were run across, around and under the Greater Caucasus chain to establish new dependency relationships. Russian oligarchs — and sometimes the Russian state — were encouraged to purchase key pieces of infrastructure from the perennially cash-strapped Armenia and Georgia. By 2007, Russian entities owned all of Armenia's energy, rail and telecommunications assets (among many others). Russia even owns an Iranian-financed and -built natural gas line connecting Armenia to Iran. Russian grain supplies now account for the bulk of the diets of all of the Caucasus people save Azerbaijan. And, of course, Russian financial largess remains a reason why the separatist enclaves of Abkhazia, South Ossetia and Nagorno-Karabakh continue to exist at all.

As of the summer of 2008, no one denied that Russian power south of the Greater Caucasus was strong, but by the end of the year, it became clear that Russian power was irresistible. In August 2008, rising tensions between Tbilisi and the separatist enclave of South Ossetia broke into full war. Within hours, Russian troops already prepositioned in anticipation of the conflict poured through the Roki tunnel, the route under the Greater Caucasus connecting Russia and South Ossetia. The Russian military demonstrated the fundamental ability to exercise military force in its periphery to establish military realities on the ground and achieve larger political ends.

Russian "peacekeepers" already stationed in Abkhazia and South Ossetia coordinated with local Abkhaz and Ossetian militias to attack a number of Georgian positions in northwestern and northern Georgia. Even Russian air force assets in Armenia were used. Within five days, Russian forces had broken the Georgian state into multiple, disconnected pieces. In the end, Russia did not destroy Georgia, but its reinforcing of Abkhazia and South Ossetia — and Moscow's formal recognition of their independence — entrenched Russian power south of the Greater Caucasus within easy striking distance of Georgia's major ports, the Baku-Tbilisi-Ceyhan corridor and the Georgian capital. Essentially, the Kremlin gained the perennial ability to threaten to physically isolate Tbilisi from the coast and cut the country in half.

Besides eliminating Georgia as significant threat to Russian power, the war had several profound and immediate implications.

First, at home and abroad, it became obvious that Russia had shaken off the pall of the First Chechen War and was willing and able to use military force to secure its interests. This did as much to regenerate Russian confidence as the First Gulf War did to regenerate American confidence in 1991.

Second, the war terrified the Azerbaijani government, which until then had been considering a Georgia-style, incremental increase of pressure on Nagorno-Karabakh. With the Russians so clearly and forcefully putting the military option on the table, Baku was forced to evaluate the Russian military presence in Armenia in a new light.

Third, the former Soviet states had to consider that Russian power was sufficiently strong and omnipresent to overwhelm what lingering and erratic attention the Americans were willing to dedicate to the region. Kazakhstan, Belarus, Kyrgyzstan, Tajikistan and Turkmenistan all dialed back their efforts to resist Russian encroachment. Moldova and Uzbekistan shifted from an indifferent or partially hostile stance regarding Russian power to neutrality.

Finally, the war was a not-so-subtle dig at NATO, some members of which considered Georgia to be a candidate for membership. No direct NATO assistance whatsoever was provided during the war. All the United States proved willing or able to do was make a symbolic deployment of destroyers to the Black Sea and airlift the Georgian contingent in Iraq back to the Caucasus so they could fight for their homeland. NATO's lack of activity greatly diminished the alliance's aura throughout the region and even made full member states such as Estonia, Latvia and Lithuania wonder if their formal security guarantees would be honored should the Russians target them. Many of the newer NATO member states have since moderated their positions on Russian power as a result.

Since the August 2008 war, Russian power has reached a post-Soviet high. Belarus and Kazakhstan have been reintegrated into the Russian economy via a Soviet-style customs union. Russian intelligence has reworked the internal politics of Ukraine and Kyrgyzstan, helping to undo the color revolutions and returning pro-Russian governments to power. Russian forces have been deployed in larger numbers to Armenia and Tajikistan, solidifying Moscow's grip on their future.

As of 2011, the Russians consider the Caucasus region — Greater and intra both — solved. Western power — while not precisely excised — is certainly unable to function independent of the Russian rubric. Iran's power plays into Azerbaijan are seen as low-key and cultural, and therefore tolerable as they are not perceived to be challenging the Russian position. Turkey's recent attempts to heal relations with Armenia — whose foreign policy and strategic planning is wholly handled by Moscow — have dealt substantial damage to Turkey's relationship with each state. So long as the United States continues to be busy with the Muslim world, Moscow remains secure in its military domination of its Northern Caucasus republics and its political influence of the region as a whole.

ETHNICITIES OF THE CAUCASUS

Legend:
- Georgians
- Chechen
- Abkhaz
- Armenians
- Kurds
- Ossetians
- Azerbaijani
- Ingush
- Russian
- Turkish
- Other or mixed
- Sparsely populated

0 mi   100   200
0 km

RUSSIA

UKRAINE

KAZAKHSTAN

TURKMENISTAN

Black Sea

Caspian Sea

GEORGIA

AZERBAIJAN

ARMENIA

AZ.

TURKEY

IRAN

Copyright STRATFOR 2011   www.STRATFOR.com

CHAPTER 9:
Georgia: The Would-Be Fourth Power

Georgia has the most robust ethnic identity of the region's three minor states. Geographic access limitations caused by the Greater and Lesser Caucasus ranges, combined with the general disinterest of outsiders in using the intra-Caucasus region as a trade route, have allowed the Georgians to live in relative isolation compared to the myriad other ethnicities that make the Caucasus region their home. The lands of western Georgia are also the most fertile and well watered of the broader region, historically granting Georgia more stable natural population dynamics than even the three major powers that surround the Caucasus. (The Eurasian steppe and Anatolian and Persian highlands are all predominantly arid and historically have received erratic amounts of rainfall.) Finally, Georgia abuts the Black Sea coast, which gives its population access to the wider world — albeit truncated due to the Turkish Straits — a unique characteristic for a Caucasus people.

But a strong identity hardly means that Georgia is — or ever has been — a significant power. Any entity strong enough to project power into the intra-mountain zone can by definition destroy any Georgian state. The economic benefits of the Black Sea coast, the agricultural stability of the western plains and barriers of the Greater and Lesser Caucasus Mountains simply are not enough to make Georgia independent, wealthy and secure.

The only opportunity the Georgians have to exercise any kind of independence is when the lands in all three approaches to the Caucasus are disunited or preoccupied with other concerns. This

ETHNICITIES OF GEORGIA

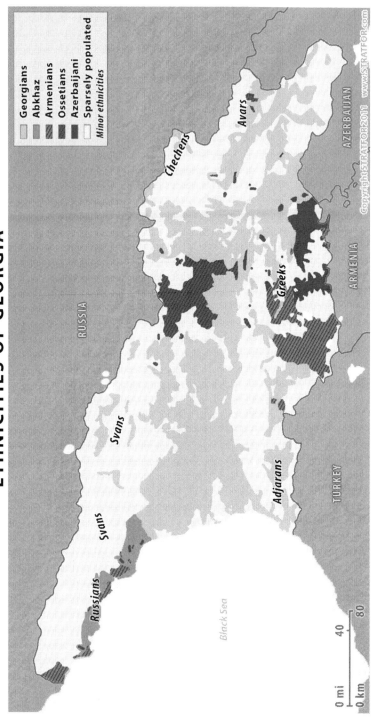

happened briefly in the 1990s, immediately after World War I, and most famously in the Georgian mind during the 12th and 13th centuries when a brief period of Georgian power resulted in a local renaissance, which actually preceded (and in the Georgian mind, influenced) the European Renaissance. This golden age was made possible by the collapse of Byzantium and the Seljuk Empire, which created power vacuums in Persia and Anatolia. The age abruptly ended when the Mongols swarmed the region and beyond. With very few exceptions thereafter, extra-Caucasus powers took their turns ruling Georgia in whole or in part, with the three most recognized powers being Persia, Ottoman Turkey and Russia. Georgian history is replete with examples of great battles and harsh occupations as these outside powers have come and gone from the region.

Dealing with the larger powers, however, is only part of the problem — and the only part of the problem the Georgians wish to discuss. The other half of the picture is that Georgians are hardly the only Caucasus peoples, even within the territory of modern-day Georgia. There are dozens of deep mountain valleys that empty into the Georgian lowlands, each home to its own ethnicity or mix of ethnicities. These include, but are hardly limited to, Adjarans, Abkhaz, Ossetians, Chechens, Greeks, Jews, Tatars, Laz, Megrelians and Svans. Even when Georgia has been strong, it has never been strong enough to absorb or defeat all of these smaller groups.

These two characteristics combined have had a peculiar impact on the Georgian psyche. The (relative) blessings of geography have ingrained in Georgians the belief that they can be a significant power in their own right, and they proudly point to a number of periods in history when they have indeed stood on their own. But Georgia's inability to make these periods of strength last are not blamed so much on the simple fact that they cannot win in a contest against the region's major players but instead upon the smaller nations that Georgians see as being in league with those major players. The Georgians believe that if only the smaller nations would do as they were told, Georgia would be able to resist outside pressure.

The result is a country that feels superior to everyone around it. The Georgians harbor a grudge toward the mountain peoples because the Georgians see them as hobbling the country's ability to achieve greatness. Georgia is bitter toward Azerbaijan and Armenia because the Georgians see them as all too willing to submit to the authority of Turkey, Iran and Russia. And of course Georgia is resentful toward the big three powers, which it sees as infringing cruelly upon Georgian sovereignty. In contemporary times, this mindset has been reinforced by the presence of the United States. Georgia's access to the Black Sea has given it hope that an extra-regional player could help alter the Caucasus power dynamic. Indeed, during the Russian nadir in the late 1990s and early 2000s, it appeared that the United States would join the regional three major powers in the Caucasus contest and become an external guarantor of Georgian sovereignty just as the United States did for Western Europe during the Cold War. But Washington's preoccupation with the Islamic world, combined with a steady Russian resurgence, ended this possibility. What it did not end was Tbilisi's hope for that possibility.

In times when one or more of the big three powers eclipse Georgian power, this mindset often results in unmitigated policy failures. Not only can Georgia not stand up to any of them, its penchant for self-aggrandizement inhibits its ability to play the three off each other. Georgia normally only attempts to play the balance-of-power game when it has already become painfully clear that it has been outclassed, and by that time it is typically too late. The August 2008 war with Russia is a case in point. Any unbiased outsider realized months before the war began that no one was going to come to Tbilisi's aid, yet Georgian strategic policy was clearly intended to provoke a conflict so that outside powers — the United States, NATO and Turkey, in that order — would intervene and firmly eject Russian influence from the region. It was an unrealistic policy built upon unrealistic expectations, and its failure resulted in the de facto breaking of the Georgian state.

SECESSIONIST REGIONS

Copyright STRATFOR 2011   www.STRATFOR.com

CHAPTER 10:
Georgia's Secessionist Regions

In Georgia, the many river valleys in the Greater and Lesser Caucasus have created pockets of populations that see themselves as independent from Tbilisi. This has led to the rise of four main secessionist or separatist regions in Georgia, which account for approximately 30 percent of the country's area and 20 percent of its population.

The smaller two of these four regions are on Georgia's southern border — Adjara on the border with Turkey and Samtskhe-Javakheti on the border with Armenia. Adjarans are considered a sub-group of the broader Georgian ethnicity and have never formally declared independence, nor have they battled with the Georgians in the post-Cold War era. What they have done, however, is exist in de facto independence within the framework of the Georgian state. The region is critical to Georgia's sustainability. It is home to Georgia's second-largest port and primary road route to Turkey, making Adjara Georgia's window on the world and the richest portion of the country. The Georgians were able to put down an Adjaran uprising in 2004 with such effectiveness that Tbilisi managed to oust the pro-Russian Adjaran government; however, the population is still widely pro-Russian.

Samtskhe-Javakheti is a landlocked region with a majority Armenian population. Yerevan has held considerable sway in the region — even before the end of the Soviet period, and in the post-Cold War era Russia often projects power into Samtskhe-Javakheti via the Armenian state. Tbilisi is more desperate to keep control over this area than it is Adjara. The two major intra-Caucasus energy pipelines — the Baku-Tbilisi-Ceyhan oil pipeline and the South Caucasus natural gas pipeline — travel through the mountains of Samtskhe-Javakheti into Turkey. Transit fees generated by those lines together constitute the single largest source of income for the Georgian national government. Samtskhe-Javakheti has called for autonomy, like Georgia's other three secessionist regions, but it has never raised arms against Tbilisi. Unlike Adjara, it has never held de facto independence.

The remaining two separatist regions, Abkhazia and South Ossetia, are another matter entirely. The Abkhaz are a distinct Caucasus ethnicity populating Georgia's northwestern extremity, living on the thin coastal strip that links Georgia with Russia. The South Ossetians live in a single, broad valley in north-central Georgia and share a common background with the Ossetians of the Russian republic of North Ossetia. Both groups have regularly clashed with Georgian authorities throughout their history, and in recent centuries both have been fervently pro-Russian in order to gain an ally against the Georgians.

During the Soviet collapse, both regions erupted into ethnic violence and eventually full-scale war. In 1989, South Ossetia declared unification with North Ossetia in Russia, which set it on the road to war with Georgia in 1991. Clashes between Georgians and Abkhaz also flared up in 1989, developing into a war in 1992. As a course of the two wars, both regions declared and achieved de facto independence from Georgia through a high level of autonomy and permanent stationing of Russian troops.

These two wars of independence shared three aspects that continue to shape the region. First, the wars' results severed direct economic connections between Georgia and Russia, greatly accelerating and deepening the depression that affected Georgia in the 1990s. South Ossetia controls the southern end of the Roki tunnel, the only tunnel through the Greater Caucasus. Abkhazia sits on the only rail line directly linking Georgia and Russia, and the Abkhaz port of Sukhumi is Georgia's largest port.

Second, the conflicts were a warm-up for much of the fighting that has plagued the region in the years since. There were more combatants in the two wars than just the Abkhaz, Ossetians and Georgians. All of the various groups that were considering launching their own independence movements sent forces to participate on one side or another to hone their skills. The groups participating included Nagorno-Karabakh's Armenians, North Ossetians, Chechens, Ingush and various smaller groups.

Third — and from the Georgians' point of view, most importantly — the Russians were not idle bystanders, and they did not limit their assistance to weapons supplies to the regions. Regular Russian forces participated in both conflicts, even providing air cover for the secessionists at some points. Following the wars, the Russian-dominated Commonwealth of Independent States (CIS) stationed 1,000-2,500 peacekeepers in both regions; both forces were there to deter Georgia from attempting to recapture the territories.

Aside from a handful of expulsions to remove most of the ethnic Georgian populations from both regions, very little changed in either Abkhazia or South Ossetia until 2008. In August of that year, South Ossetian forces baited the Georgians by shelling Georgian villages on the outskirts of the South Ossetian capital of Tshkinvali. Georgian government retaliated by launching an attack on the city. Russian forces, which had been prepared for this sequence of events, began streaming through the Roki tunnel within hours of the Georgian attack. Shortly thereafter, Russian-coordinated Abkhaz and South Ossetian forces targeted a multitude of Georgian positions on the borders of Abkhaz and South Ossetian territory, while Russian troops moved deep into the central and western portions of Georgia proper.

Within eight days, Georgia had been routed, the oil and natural gas transport lines had been cut, the Georgian port of Poti had been captured, and Russian forces were poised to attack Tbilisi itself. Russia formally recognized the independence of Abkhazia and South Ossetia and quickly enacted mutual defense agreements with both, formalizing the CIS peacekeeping brigades into regular military units and bolstering those units' forces to a combined 7,000.

Tbilisi knows it can do little about the Russian military on its territory. Its problem is rooted in the old Soviet occupation system. Whereas the intelligence apparatus was responsible for controlling the bulk of the country during the Soviet era, the intra-Caucasus region was also a military frontier with Iran and Turkey. It would not do to have a region under de facto military occupation supplying forces to the military that was doing the occupying. Not only did Georgia, Armenia and Azerbaijan lack internal militaries, they also had no local military tradition. In many ways, the Georgians' wars with Abkhazia and South Ossetia were as bungled as Russia's first war with Chechnya.

The years of independence during the 1990s actually deepened this military inability, and not simply because of a shortage of funds. Rather than begin developing a military appropriate to national needs, Tbilisi instead set its sights on NATO membership with the explicit plan of making itself as useful to the United States as possible. Investments were made into civilian-military relations, long-range and long-term deployments as part of NATO battalions, peace-keeping and reconstruction efforts — all the sort of things that the Americans needed as part of the various Balkan peacekeeping operations in the 1990s. Georgia was also among the first states friendly to the United States to volunteer forces, however modest, to assist in the Iraqi occupation and eventually in the Afghan war. In contrast, what Georgia needed to fight its wars was experience with armor and artillery, along with anti-aircraft technologies that would make the Russians think twice before supporting Abkhazia and South Ossetia.

In short, the Georgian gamble was to hope that Washington would be so enamored with Tbilisi that NATO membership would be achieved and the Americans would assist Georgia in reclaiming Abkhazia and South Ossetia. In August 2008, the Georgian gamble failed.

Since the Russo-Georgian war, little has changed. There has been some light discussion within Tbilisi of modernizing the Georgian military to address domestic needs, be that fighting secessionist regions or defending against the Russians. The problem has been

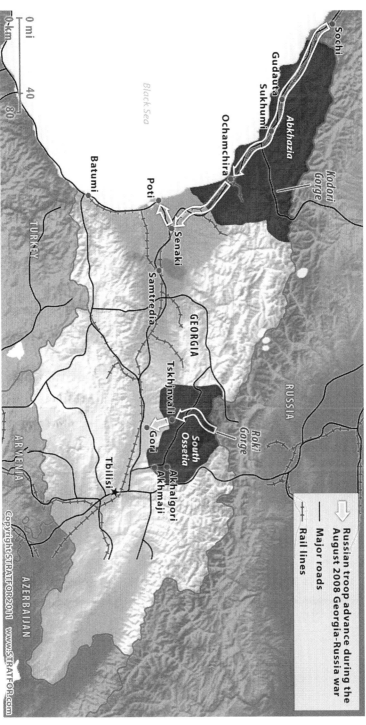

RUSSIA-GEORGIA WAR, AUGUST 2008

Russian troop advance during the August 2008 Georgia-Russia war

— Major roads

‡‡ Rail lines

Sochi

Gudauta
Sukhumi

Abkhazia

Ochamchira

Kodori
Gorge

Black Sea

Batumi

Poti

Senaki

Samtredia

TURKEY

GEORGIA

Tskhinvali

South
Ossetia

Gori

Akhalgori
Akhmaji

Roki
Gorge

RUSSIA

Tbilisi

ARMENIA

AZERBAIJAN

0 mi
40
80

0 km

technology acquisition and training, and that leads invariably to the Americans and their concerns, which are twofold.

First, the United States simply does not trust the Georgians not to contribute to the start of another military conflict. The Americans are fully aware that the August 2008 war put Washington's security guarantees — ultimately the basis of the NATO alliance structure — into doubt. Thus, while the United States continues indirectly to support Georgia via the IMF and World Bank, it shies away from supplying equipment to the Georgians that it cannot expressly control.

Second, the Americans need the Russians right now far more than they need the Georgians. U.S. efforts in the Middle East depend in part on the Russians not providing too many nuclear and military technologies to the Iranians. The United States also needs Russia's help in logistical support for Afghanistan. Part of the price for Russian cooperation on Iran and Afghanistan is American cooperation on Georgia. Technology — and money — still flows from the United States to Georgia, but no longer in the amounts seen in the 1990s. That leaves Georgia limited to seeking equipment on the international market — a market that requires payments in hard currency that Tbilisi finds very hard to acquire, and a market that is wary of the political cost of supplying Georgia against Russia's very determined wishes.

CHAPTER 11:
Azerbaijan: Resigned to Pragmatism

Azerbaijan has few of the geographic advantages of Georgia. Its lands are mostly semi-arid rather than well watered, greatly limiting its population growth until investments in industrialized agriculture were made in during the Soviet era. Its coast is on the Caspian, a landlocked sea with northern reaches — the one place with navigable river access — that freeze in the winter, sharply limiting trade opportunities.

The coastal plain connecting Azerbaijan to the Eurasian steppe is considerably wider and shorter than the long, narrow plain connecting the Georgian lowlands to the Eurasian steppe. This allows any northern power to access the eastern lowlands more easily than the western lowlands. There is far easier access for southern powers as well, as the eastern lowlands directly abut the Persian highlands. The result is a culture that is both more fearful and more flexible than the Georgians.

The Georgians are convinced that they would succeed as an independent power if not for outside support for the various minor nations attached to the western flatlands. After all, many of these groups live near Georgia's major population centers or even have some degree of control over Georgian access to the wider world. The South Ossetians have the ability to use artillery against the outskirts of Tbilisi, while the Abkhaz completely control the main rail line out of the country, and the Adjarans hold Georgia's most economically significant port. Georgian fear is reserved primarily for these various groups, and Tbilisi attempts to monitor all of them.

A CRUCIBLE OF NATIONS

In contrast, the eastern intra-mountain flatlands of Azerbaijan have far fewer minor nations because they have far fewer mountain fastnesses — only one is noteworthy, and it does not threaten Baku's writ over its core territory. The area is Nagorno-Karabakh, and its resident Armenians achieved de facto independence in their 1988-1994 war. Since the cease-fire, they have remained secluded in their mountain fastness in the country's west. The Azerbaijanis would obviously prefer to regain the territory, but its loss has little functional impact upon Azerbaijan's fate.

The only other groups that Baku is concerned with are the Lezgins and, to a lesser degree, the Avars of the Greater Caucasus. The vast majority of both groups live in the unstable Russian republic of Dagestan, with a few residing in northeastern Azerbaijan. Both populations are Sunni, with the Lezgins having a reputation for being radical, in terms of both religiosity and violence, as well as a penchant for guerilla warfare. Here the issue is not so much irredentism as it is security and political chaos. Baku is concerned that spillover from Dagestan will fray its control over its northern border, but this is more a law-enforcement concern akin to American concerns over its Mexican borderland than a fear of secession.

Azerbaijan's preoccupying concern is not that outside powers might leverage these groups to destroy Azerbaijan but instead that foreign influence will affect the Azerbaijanis directly. It is a reasonable fear. The ease with which outside powers can reach the eastern flatlands has resulted in the Azerbaijanis' partial assimilation at numerous stages throughout their history. Within the past four centuries, Azerbaijanis have been assimilated by Persia, Turkey and Russia. There was even a brief period in the late 1990s when American culture had a moment in Baku.

Somewhat ironically, this awareness of their vulnerability makes the Azerbaijanis more flexible than the Georgians. Because they are so exposed to outside influence, because they lack the access to the Black Sea that gives the Georgians the hope of an extra-regional savior and because their territory has so few national building blocks,

Azerbaijanis do not stubbornly deny the inevitability of foreigners affecting their land and people.

Georgians' trademark characteristics of defiance and superiority are based on unrealistic assumptions about their geopolitical position, while the Azerbaijanis' more realistic understanding of their lack of choices resigns them to pragmatism. In Georgia, the result is resistance until collapse, while in Azerbaijan the result is efforts at compromise and even collusion. Azerbaijanis realize that they have little choice but to seek a suzerainty relationship with whichever major regional power happens to be in ascendance.

It is worth noting that suzerainty is not surrender. Azerbaijan's much more accurate read of its position — weaknesses and all — allows Baku to play the balance-of-power game much more effectively than Tbilisi does, using its relations with each of the three major powers to manage the others.

In contemporary times, Azerbaijan defers to Moscow's wishes, and as such has at times become a tool of Russian foreign policy: It remained scrupulously neutral during the 2008 Georgia-Russia war and serves as a leading transfer point for Russian gasoline flowing to Iran in direct defiance of American foreign policy goals. But Moscow's overriding presence puts limits on Iran's efforts to influence anti-government groups in Azerbaijan. Turkey's somewhat naive belief that all Azerbaijanis simply wish to be Turks gives Baku an effective tool to limit Moscow's demands somewhat. And so long as Baku can keep the major three regional powers maneuvering against each other, it can carve out just enough room to bring in Western energy firms to develop its oil and natural gas potential, granting it an economic base it would have otherwise lacked. It is far from a perfect arrangement, but considering Baku's neighborhood the fact that it even enjoys nominal independence is no small achievement.

CHAPTER 12:
Armenia: Independence in Name Only

Armenia must be considered separately from the other two minor Caucasus states, as its history is much less geographically anchored than Georgia's, Azerbaijan's or those of the myriad small nations in the intra-mountain zone. In part, this is because Armenia is not actually in the intra-mountain zone, located instead on the south side of the Lesser Caucasus. It is a bit of a misnomer to consider Armenia as in the Caucasus region at all — in fact, contemporary Armenia is more properly placed at the extreme eastern edge of the Anatolian highlands.

Armenia is not a nation-state in the traditional sense, and the Armenians are atypical of nations as well.

The Armenians can be described more accurately as a semi-nomadic people who have lived conterminously with many other peoples over the centuries. Armenia's history is not that of an entity that expands and shrinks (Russia, Turkey, Persia) or fondly recalls periods in which its borders expanded wildly if briefly (Georgia, Azerbaijan, Serbia, Bulgaria, Mongolia). Instead, the entire zone of governance has actually moved. This is hardly surprising, as unlike the Georgians and Azerbaijanis, the two Caucasus chains did not shield the Armenians. Consequently, the core lands of the various Armenian states through the ages have actually been in different locations.

The current incarnation of Armenia is perhaps the most awkward. Aside from the Lesser Caucasus to its north, it has no natural boundary defining its borders, and aside from the semi-fertile region to the west and south of Lake Sevan it has no true national core like

ARMENIA'S RANGE

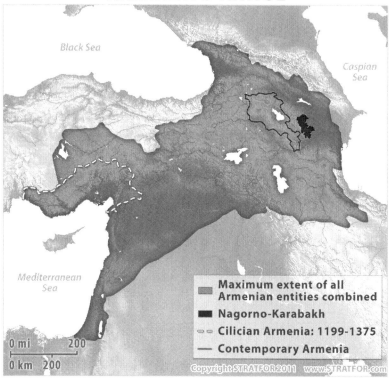

the intra-mountain lowlands that form Georgia and Azerbaijan, or the Sea of Marmara region that anchors Turkey. The valley in which the capital, Yerevan, is located is actually split between four states: Armenia, Azerbaijan, Iran and Turkey.

While Georgia and Azerbaijan have spent most of their history as subunits of or thralls to larger empires, the Armenians have lived most of their even longer history without a state in any form. As long-time stateless people they have either fled or been relocated based on the needs and actions of the larger powers in their neighborhood. Like other stateless groups, the result is a diaspora that far outnumbers the population of what is now the nation-state of Armenia. The power of the political and economic Armenian elite reflects this scattering. The Armenian elite wield power in places far removed from the lands of the Armenians' origin — such as in France and the United States — rather than in modern-day Armenia. This is hardly a new development. Before modern times the last Armenian state was the Cilicia incarnation, centered on the modern city of Turkey's Ceyhan, in the 13th and 14th centuries — a state whose borders have zero overlap with present-day "independent" Armenia.

It is worth explaining why we put the word "independent" in quotation marks. The Armenians assert that in 1915 the Turks carried out a genocide expressly to wipe out the Armenian population in Anatolia. The Turks counter that the Armenian view takes the events of 1915 out of context and that Armenians ignore the effects of World War I, a civil war and famine. Regardless of the charges or counter-charges, what both sides agree on is that Armenian populations and influence ceased to be a factor within the borders of what eventually morphed into the modern Turkish republic in 1923. This left the largest remaining concentration of Armenians both trapped within what eventually became the Soviet Union and utterly separated from other remnant Armenian communities in the Middle East.

The implications of this for the Armenian nation were dire. As of 1915, the Armenians had been a stateless people for over five centuries, and as such, their elite were geographically scattered. The events of 1915-1923 destroyed or displaced their single largest geographic concentration, with the obvious impact upon the coherence of what elites remained in Anatolia. The largest remnants of this group were then subsumed into a totalitarian government that tolerated very little local autonomy, effectively destroying what little elite remained. For the next 75 years, Soviet Armenia was ruled without influence from the outside world, much less from the elite of the Armenian diaspora.

In 1991, Armenia attained independence for the first time since the 14th century. That independence was, for all practical purposes, stillborn. Immediately upon independence, landlocked Armenia fought a war with Azerbaijan over Nagorno-Karabakh, suffered an embargo from Turkey and was forced to make due with cool-to-cold relations with both Georgia and Iran. Faced with such an unmitigated national disaster, it is no surprise that Armenia was the one former Soviet state that did not even attempt to eject Russian forces, seeing them (rightly) as its one possible lifeline. Consequently, Russian influence — if not outright control — over Armenian security policy never waned in the post-Cold War era. Similar scenarios played out in the other Caucasus regions where stateless people found themselves under severe military stress — most notably in the Georgian regions of Abkhazia, South Ossetia and Adjara.

As Russia recovered from its post-Cold War collapse, Russia's dominating presence in all of these entities evolved into firm, strong military commitments utterly independent from one another. For Armenia, this formalized the separation between Armenia proper and Nagorno-Karabakh. Rather than a united front that might have led to a Greater Armenia, Armenian authorities in both entities now serve as separate — and somewhat mutually suspicious — tools of Russian strategic planning. The current setup codifies both Armenia's status as a Russian satellite state and Nagorno-Karabakh's status as a Russian proxy and allows Moscow more flexibility in playing the various Caucasus power groups against each other.

CHAPTER 13:
Armenian-Azerbaijani Disputes

Armenia is a geographic oddity in the Caucasus, as it lacks the sharp delineations of the lands that host most of the other peoples in the region. This characteristic has fueled territorial disputes.

Most Armenians in the Caucasus live in a portion of a single broad mountain valley split roughly in four between Armenia (northeast), Turkey (northwest), Iran (southwest) and Azerbaijan (southeast). The Hrazdan River constitutes the northern limit of the valley and joins the Aras River, which flows in from Turkey, just south of Yerevan. At that point, Armenia's territory ends; the western bank of the Aras is part of Iran, and the eastern bank belongs to the Azerbaijani exclave of Nakhchivan. The four portions do not have any meaningful geographic insulation from one another. This corridor, called the Zangezur Corridor, is between the Lesser Caucasus to the northeast, the highlands of Anatolia to the southwest and the Zagros Mountains of Persia to the south.

The Zangezur Corridor's complex political geography is not new. Understanding its division is crucial to understanding the first of two regions disputed between Armenia and Azerbaijan.

Nakhchivan

Nakhchivan is a landlocked exclave of Azerbaijan. As an exclave, it shares no land connection with Azerbaijan, instead being sandwiched between Armenia to the north and Iran to the south, while sharing a tiny border with Turkey to the west. Geographically, Nakhchivan is much simpler to describe: it is the southeastern portion of the Zangezur Corridor.

Nakhchivan was part of every major empire that has ever existed in the region. Its strategic value is easy to understand when one looks at a topographic map: The Zangezur Corridor is by far the largest valley in the region where Anatolia, the Zagros Mountains and the Lesser Caucasus blur together. Nakhchivan, as the southeastern extreme of that corridor, is the portion most likely to be the subject of competition for anyone wanting to come to or from the Persian core. Persia and Turkey have fought over the region for centuries, with Russia joining the competition seriously in the 1800s. Whoever controls the Zangezur Corridor has the ability to project power into the Turkish and Russian spheres of influence and into the Persian core territories.

For Armenia, Nakhchivan is about both strategy and identity. The Armenians believe that they are the direct descendants of the Biblical Noah, whose ark is broadly agreed to have settled on the slopes of Mount Ararat. Ararat is within Turkey's borders, but the Armenians still claim it as their national symbol. For the most part, in the Armenian mythos, Noah's family — the first Armenians — settled in the lands that straddle the Armenia-Nakhchivan border.

The region spent most of the past millennia as part of either Persia or Ottoman Turkey (with an occasional Russian interruption), but in the time between the destruction of the Ottoman Empire in World War I and the rise of the Soviet Union, Nakhchivan entered a chaotic period. During a rash of Caucasus conflicts, Nakhchivan was sometimes ruled by Armenia, sometimes ruled by Azerbaijan and sometimes an independent state. This came to an end when the Soviet Army invaded, crushing local governments and declaring that there were no borders, and thus no conflicts, between "Soviet brother states."

Yet even with such declarations, the territory had to fall under one regional government or the other, and Josef Stalin ultimately made the lasting decision. In the 1920s, Stalin was Commissar of Nationalities, which meant he was in charge of bringing the peoples of the Transcaucasus into the Soviet cultural fold. One of his most-used strategies was redrawing or solidifying disputed borders to maximize potential ethnic strife so that, should the various pieces of the Soviet Union ever gain independence, they would be far more concerned with fighting each other than challenging their former master.

Stalin, always with his eye on potential rivals, discussed the details of his Sovietization programs with the newly republican Turks. In the 1920s, the Soviets had no desire to do battle with the Turks, who were busy reconsolidating their territory and had no qualms about using military force to seize pieces of territory they felt were theirs — most notably ejecting the Greeks from western Anatolia and the Syrians from Hatay. The Soviets and Turks reached an agreement that would keep both Nakhchivan and Nagorno-Karabakh under Azerbaijan's authority. That decision still haunts the region.

In contemporary times, the demography of Nakhchivan is 99 percent Azerbaijani, but it was not always that way. The Persians were the region's rulers in the 1700s and comprised most of the population, with the largest minority being Azerbaijanis. When the Russians pushed into the region in force in the 1800s, they sought to ally with their "fellow Christians" the Armenians, whom they pledged would soon rule the entire Caucasus region. Thus, throughout the 1800s the Persians were steadily replaced with Armenians, who made up about half of the population at their height. But then Stalin's machinations upturned the demographic balance again and set the region on the road to Azerbaijani domination. Much of the contemporary Azerbaijani leadership — including the ruling Aliyev dynasty — hails from the exclave.

When the Soviet Army ceased occupying the Caucasus and full war broke out between Armenia and Azerbaijan, that war quickly spread to Nakhchivan. Two factors preserved it as part of Azerbaijan. First, Nakhchivan was a front-line Soviet military location on the borders of both Iran and Turkey. As such it boasted impressive defensive fortifications and numerous weapons depots. Second, the Turks warned the Armenians that if they were serious about attacking an Azerbaijani exclave that the Turks shared a border with, the Armenians would have a larger war on their hands.

Nagorno-Karabakh

Nagorno-Karabakh is the most contentious piece of property between Baku and Yerevan. As in Nakhchivan, the Armenians had long had a foothold in Nagorno-Karabakh. Also like Nakhchivan, the region's modern history begins in the mid-18th century when the Russians first projected power into the Caucasus.

When the Russian Empire first moved into the Caucasus in force, the czars decreed that the Armenians would be the sole rulers of the region, thinking that since the Armenians were Christians, it would be easier to bridge the ethnic divide with them than it would be with the Azerbaijanis. During the Ottoman-Soviet interregnum both groups temporary lost control of the area, with the British even controlling it for a brief period as part of the post-World War I settlement. The British left the region to the Armenians, but after a series of skirmishes with Azerbaijani forces Yerevan agreed to allow Azerbaijani rule. The thinking in Yerevan was that a Russian return to the area was both inevitable and imminent, and that at such time the Russians would return control over Nagorno-Karabakh — and hopefully other territories — to Armenia.

The Armenians did not anticipate Stalin's pact with the Turks. And so, despite a strongly Armenian-majority population and strong cultural ties to Armenian entities, Nagorno-Karabakh was kept under Azerbaijan's control. Racial tensions between these groups remained high throughout the Soviet period.

Of the various parts of the former Soviet Union where violence erupted during the Soviet collapse, Nagorno-Karabakh was probably the least surprising. Social discontent and outbursts of violence plagued the region as soon as glasnost and perestroika became guiding policies, and in 1988, the region's leadership declared independence with the intent of merging with Armenia. Moscow restrained Baku from taking full military action against its wayward province, which was already involved in conflicts. But that stabilization attempt evaporated as the Soviet Union entered its death throes. Skirmishes

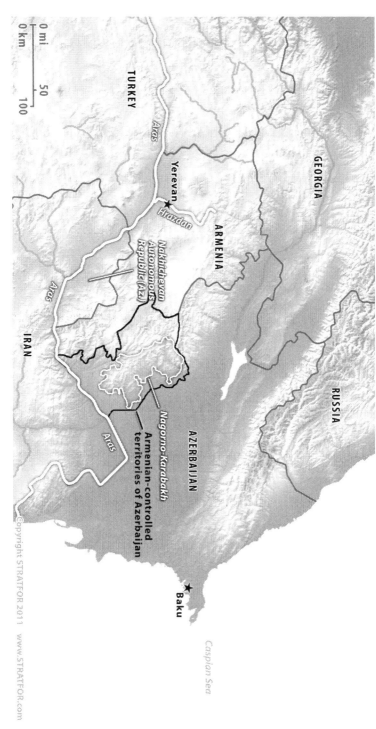

NAGORNO-KARABAKH

TURKEY

Aras

GEORGIA

Yerevan
Hrazdan

ARMENIA

Nakhichevan
Autonomous
Republic (Az.)

Aras

IRAN

RUSSIA

Aras

Nagorno-Karabakh
Armenian-controlled
territories of Azerbaijan

AZERBAIJAN

Baku

Caspian Sea

0 mi
0 km
50
100

that had been going on for three years erupted into full war in late 1991.

The outside aid given to each side during the war defined current Armenian and Azerbaijani foreign policy. There is much evidence that Azerbaijan received military aid and support from Turkey. Armenia received large sums of cash from the large Armenian diaspora, especially Armenians in the United States. Fearing a two-front war with Azerbaijan and Turkey, Armenia panicked and turned to the only power it could: Russia. Many of the former Soviet states were creating a new alliance called the Commonwealth of Independent States (CIS), which both Armenia and Azerbaijan joined. CIS "peacekeepers" were sent to Armenia in 1992, but the mainly Russian forces did more than simply peacekeeping. Azerbaijan charges that Russian and Armenian forces ended up incorporating heavily in 1992. The alliance between the two still exists.

The war raged with few breaks until 1994, when Russia brokered a cease-fire. The Nagorno-Karabakh War resulted in Armenian forces occupying roughly one-fifth of Azerbaijan's territory, a situation that has persisted. Legally, Nagorno-Karabakh is internationally recognized as part of Azerbaijan. Operationally, however, post-Soviet Baku has never held any influence in the region.

As one might expect after a war that was largely ethnic in nature, tensions remain high between Armenia and Azerbaijan — higher than tensions between any other two former Soviet republics.

There are three reasons the Nagorno-Karabakh conflict has remained frozen despite these simmering hostilities. First, the Armenians have what they want: Nagorno-Karabakh is de facto independent from Baku. So aside from the odd skirmish, the Armenians have no reason to launch military action. Even with Russian support it is difficult to envision a scenario in which the Armenians — who the Azerbaijanis outnumber nearly 3:1 — would descend from their mountainous terrain and attack the Azerbaijani lowlands.

Second is the simple issue of capacity. The Nagorno-Karabakh War was fought with Soviet weapons stockpiles. Despite much weaponry pouring in from former Soviet and Warsaw Pact states during the war, by 1994 there simply was not a lot of materiel left, and neither side had the economic capacity to purchase more. Refugee flows also contributed to the economic cost of the war. More than a million Armenians and Azerbaijanis found themselves on the wrong side of the front lines when the war began. Willingly or not, nearly all of them relocated, creating further expenses for both countries. Azerbaijan's economy did not really start expanding until the turn of the millennium, and Armenia does not have much of an economy at all anymore, with some 40 percent of the population reduced to near-subsistence farming.

Third, while many powers wanted a proxy or ally in the region — and while Russian assistance was critical to helping the Armenians fight the war in the first place — no one wanted to underwrite an endless conflict. The one thing that Russia, the United States and Turkey have consistently agreed upon is the need to pressure both sides to refrain from renewed hostilities.

Yet this chapter of history is hardly over. The war was an ethnic conflict that served as the crucible in which contemporary Armenia and Azerbaijan were formed. The issue of Nagorno-Karabakh is now central to the identity of both Armenians and Azerbaijanis in a way it has never been before in the two peoples' history. Since the war, the two sides have descended into bickering over details inconsequential to strategic policy, but after 16 years of relative peace, changes in both countries are making renewed fighting more likely. On both sides, it comes down to changes in the military equation.

With Azerbaijan, it is all about energy. U.S. involvement in the Caucasus granted Azerbaijan a large and modern energy export industry. Oil output has increased from slightly more than 100,000 barrels per day (bpd) at independence to more than 1 million bpd in 2011 and likely 1.2 million by 2013. Natural gas output has followed a similar trajectory, and Baku hopes output will be more than 30 billion cubic meters per year by 2015. The newfound energy wealth has allowed Baku to raise the military budget from a meager $175 million as recently as 2001 to more than $2 billion in 2011, with plans to raise it to more than $3 billion within two years.

CAUCASUS STATES' MILITARY BALANCE

	ARMENIA	GEORGIA	AZERBAIJAN
2001			
Defense budget	65	22	175
GDP	1,912	3,043	5,273
Defense budget as % of GDP	3.40%	0.72%	3.32%
2010			
Defense budget	437	420	2,000
GDP	9,286	11,363	52,196
Defense budget as % of GDP	4.71%	3.70%	3.83%

Note: In million USD
Sources: International Institute for Strategic Studies and STRATFOR estimates

Azerbaijan still relies heavily on military hardware from Russia and its proxy, Belarus, but Baku also has been making plans to diversify its suppliers, looking to the NATO states and Israel. Azerbaijan is also interested in gaining licenses to begin producing its own equipment — something for which the Azerbaijanis currently have no real capability. Though Baku says it seeks to improve interoperability with NATO, its foremost goal is to expand its training regime internationally wherever and however it can in order to improve its indigenous fighting capability. This is Azerbaijan's biggest weakness: It may have been on a military spending spree, but it has no experience — particularly war-fighting experience — as a larger and more modern military.

GROSS DOMESTIC PRODUCT OF THE CAUCASUS STATES

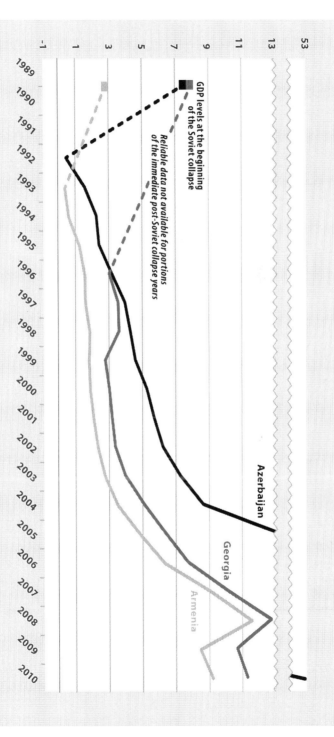

GDP levels at the beginning
of the Soviet collapse

Reliable data not available for portions
of the immediate post-Soviet collapse years

Azerbaijan

Georgia

Armenia

Sources: International Monetary Foundation and Statkomitet CIS Database

RUSSIAN MILITARY IN THE CAUCASUS

REGION	2011 PERSONNEL
Northern Caucasus	90,000*
Armenia	5,000
Azerbaijan	900
Abkhazia (Georgia)	3,800
South Ossetia (Georgia)	3,000

Note: Personnel is military forces with support staffing
*Includes Chechen Ground Forces
Source: STRATFOR's Russian Defense Sources

Thus, while Georgia wants to improve its military to meet NATO standards in order to speed Tbilisi's full alliance membership should that opportunity ever arise, Azerbaijan wants the training to ensure its military is prepared to fight a war at home. The combination of rapidly rising wealth, a rapid military buildup and friendly ties with the West and Turkey has raised Azerbaijan's confidence exponentially.

It has also triggered panic in Armenia. Of the three Caucasus states, Armenia has the weakest military. During the Nagorno-Karabakh war, the Armenians mixed their Soviet military expertise with guerilla warfare against Azerbaijan's largely unprofessional military. Now the tables have turned and Azerbaijan is building a trained, modern force, while Armenia has not been able to replace most of its military equipment since the war's end. Armenia has also seen more than 30 percent of its citizens leave the country, versus only 10 percent for Azerbaijan. The Azerbaijanis now spend more on their annual military budget than Armenia's entire national budget.

Since domestic-driven military expansion like Azerbaijan's is not an option for Armenia, Yerevan has done the next best thing and sought the assistance of its only ally: Russia. Moscow has been more than happy to entrench its military in Armenia. Russia currently maintains a force of 5,000 throughout the country, and Russian troops have been known to patrol Armenia's borders with Georgia, Azerbaijan, Iran and Turkey — something each country is well aware of. The one problem the alliance faces is that unlike other Russian-protected enclaves in other parts of the Caucasus, Armenia does not share a land border with Russia.

However, this does not mean that Russia's presence in Armenia is negligible. The problem is that Armenia and Azerbaijan both think they have an understanding with the Russians. The Azerbaijanis think that the Russians are only there to prevent Baku from launching assaults against Armenia proper and that Nagorno-Karabakh is seen as a reasonable target in Moscow's eyes. The Armenians think that the Russians are there to protect Armenian interests against all threats. Each state thinks it has the upper hand.

Azerbaijan knows its military and economy are superior to Armenia's and believes its population is fully in support of another war. Baku also believes it has an understanding that Turkey will come to Azerbaijan's aid should war break out. On the other hand, Armenia knows the Karabakh Armenians are capable warriors who have a record of ejecting Azerbaijani military power and believes the Russian presence is an unmitigated advantage that Baku cannot hope to overcome. Amid these beliefs and expectations is a conflict that is the region's most likely to erupt into fighting.

NORTHERN CAUCASUS REPUBLICS

Caspian Sea

AZERBAIJAN

Dagestan

Chechnya

Ingushetia

RUSSIA

Kabardino-Balkaria

North Ossetia

Karachay-Cherkessia

GEORGIA

ARMENIA

Adygea

TURKEY

Black Sea

0 mi   50
0 km   100

CHAPTER 14:
The Northern Caucasus

Anchoring in the Northern Caucasus has been a goal of the Russian government since the days of Muscovy, as the Greater Caucasus range is the most secure place the Russians might be able to concentrate their defensive forces. However, not only is that range far removed from Moscow, to its north are the vast, open spaces of the Eurasian steppe, which allow invaders access to the northern slopes of the range with ease. As such, the inhabitants of the Northern Caucasus have been in constant battle against foreign rule for the length of their recorded history. Over the ages, they have struggled against the Romans, Huns, Mongols, Ottomans and Russians, just to name a few. The local inhabitants have viewed the Russians as their primary foes since the Russians first began to claim the area in the 17th century.

The most powerful of the many nations that inhabit the region are the Chechens. The lowlands of the Terek River have typically given the Chechens reliable food supplies in a somewhat arid region, and the Argun and Vedeno gorges give them reliable fallback positions from which to wage guerrilla warfare. The result is a hardy and often disagreeable people who extract the maximum possible price from any entity that seeks to use their lands. For the past 200 years, that entity has been Russia.

Chechnya is only one of Russia's Northern Caucasus republics. The region as a whole is a murky ethnic stew split into seven territories: Adygea, Karachay-Cherkessia, Kabardino-Balkaria, North Ossetia, Ingushetia, Chechnya and Dagestan. Chechnya's rebellion, the nature

CHECHNYA

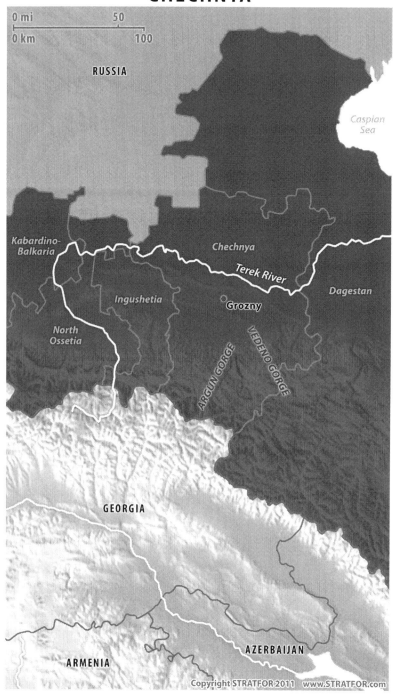

of which is both nationalist and religious — specifically Muslim — has been the most troubling to Russia. Moscow has already fought two brutal wars in the past 20 years to prevent Chechen independence, a development Russia fears would lead to Chechnya conquering or absorbing many of the other Northern Caucasus republics and eliminating the Russian anchor in the region.

To the west of Chechnya lies the republic of Ingushetia, which has tight cultural and religious links to the Chechens. Ingushetia also has both secessionist movements and movements that want Ingushetia to merge with Chechnya (whether as part of Russia or independent of it). East of Chechnya is the predominantly Muslim Dagestan. Ingushetia and Dagestan are the next two largest problem areas for Moscow. In recent years, Ingushetia's instability and militancy has been connected to Chechnya, with political and social spillover between the countries fueling radicalism. Dagestan's radicalization has been first in reaction to Chechnya, though now it is targeting Russia as well.

Kabardino-Balkaria, Karachay-Cherkessia and Adygea, the other Muslim Northern Caucasus republics, are not as volatile as Chechnya but still chafe under Russian control, only remaining Russian republics due to a constant Russian military presence. While North Ossetia, the lone Orthodox Christian province in the Northern Caucasus, is broadly pro-Russian, it still harbors nationalist sentiment that can flare up when another republic pressures it. Many in North Ossetia wish to merge with Georgia's South Ossetia and become an independent state.

As with the rest of the Caucasus, the weakening and eventual disintegration of the Soviet Union sent shock waves through the Russian Caucasus. Rivalries, turf wars, territorial disputes, religious clashes and a fight for greater autonomy — if not outright independence — sent the region spiraling into chaos.

The first inter-ethnic conflict to break out in the region was not in Chechnya but instead between Muslim Ingushetia and Orthodox North Ossetia from 1989-1991. A long rivalry between the two republics erupted into war when Ingushetia laid territorial claim to the Ossetian region of Prigorodny. Ingushetia was already unstable due to the dismemberment of the Soviet Chechen-Ingush Republic, leaving Ingushetia without any definition or legal basis for being a sovereign republic in the new Russian Federation.

Feeling unconstrained and vulnerable, the Ingush moved to assert their position in the Caucasus. This small conflict revealed the complexities in defining these regions after the fall of the Soviet Union, to keep them from clashing — or lashing out at Russian rule.

The first Chechen War from 1994-1996 defined the Russian Caucasus as wholly unstable, not simply in terms of conflicts between the various republics but also in terms of attempts to oust Russian influence — a definition maintained to this day. During the Soviet period, only 8 percent of the Soviet military was non-Slavic, and that portion was mainly made up of Muslims from Azerbaijan and Central Asians. By comparison, nearly 17 percent of the Soviet population was Muslim in the latter years of the Soviet Union. Residents of the Northern Caucasus republics were only drafted into the Soviet military in small numbers and were nearly always excluded from high command positions. The exceptions, like Chechen leader Dzokhar Dudayev, ended up leading the revolt against Russian rule. With the fall of the Soviet Union, Soviet military hardware became relatively easy to access for the militant groups in the Muslim republics. Armed with this equipment, the Muslim republics used irregular warfare, something a broken Russian security apparatus and military had little training or expertise in combating. Russian intelligence and military forces might have been trained in occupying dissident regions, but not as much in fighting guerilla warfare.

The three years between the first and second Chechen wars allowed the Chechen separatists to regroup and strengthen their ability to fight a more brutal war the second time around. Moreover, the militant organizations had expanded across the Northern Caucasus, involving fighters from Kabardino-Balkaria, North Ossetia, Ingushetia, Dagestan and more. Each group had its own style of militancy, but cross-regional clans strengthened during this period. Also, the fighting in both Ingushetia and Dagestan became nearly as dangerous as the conflict in Chechnya. The local insurgencies were starting to consolidate into a pan-North Caucasus front against the Russians.

When Putin launched the Second Chechen War in 1999, the Russian military was just starting to regroup. The first few years of fighting were merciless to the Russians. The military was still attempting to fight a modern military war against guerilla militants. The difference this time was that the Russian security services (both the Federal Security Service and Russia's foreign intelligence agency, the GRU) were starting to consolidate once again, and this shifted the momentum of the war in the early to mid-2000s.

It was during this second war that Russia began to feel the reality of large-scale and organized attacks by the Northern Caucasus militants not only in the Northern Caucasus, but also in Russia proper. A few of the most serious attacks:

- 1999: Coordinated apartment bloc bombings in Moscow, Buinaksk, and Volgodonsk blamed on Chechen militants

- Throughout the 2000s: Multiple train bombings around Moscow and St. Petersburg

- Throughout the 2000s: Multiple subway attacks in Moscow

- 2002: Moscow theater hostage crisis

- 2003: Suicide bombers outside the Kremlin

- 2004: Simultaneous destruction of two Russian airliners while in flight

- 2004: Beslan school hostage crisis that killed 380 people, mostly children

The turn to large-scale terrorist attacks by the Northern Caucasus groups changed the Russian population's view of the region. Ethnic Russians became vehemently against those from the Muslim Caucasus republics, demanding the Kremlin clamp down on them — brutally.

The reconsolidated Russian military and security services responded with their own evolution in tactics. First, they decided that instead of trying to wipe out all the militants in the region, they would target those with deeper links to the international jihadist network — those fighting for "Islamic" states and not simply independent ones. This is where those top-tier militants who were behind some of the larger terrorist attacks — such as Shamil Basayev — were eliminated. The goal was to leave those militants who had not bought into radical ideology or who were not as well connected outside of the country.

As that tactic began to give the Russians small victories, the next step was to use Russian intelligence's deep knowledge of the different power players to divide them and pit them against one another. The Kremlin started showing some of the more powerful nationalist militants that it was more lucrative to work with the Kremlin than against it. Two "reformed" militant family clans were propped up by the Kremlin: the Kadyrov family, which gained the Chechen presidency, and the Kadyrovs' rivals the Yamadayev brothers, who were put into security and political positions. The goal was to create a balance of forces under Kremlin control and to use high-ranking figures inside the militant networks to begin persuading other nationalist militants to switch sides.

By the late 2000s, the actual war began winding down. The Russian military and intelligence apparatuses were strong again, the main Islamist ideologues in the Russian Caucasus were dead, and the main nationalist militant groups were now working for the Kremlin.

There was one last surge of power from those militants left. A loose umbrella group called the Caucasus Emirates (CE) began to form in 2007. The CE was run by militant leader Doku Umarov and was intended to appoint five or more leaders for the Northern Caucasus republics (for example, a leader for Chechnya, one for Ingushetia and North Ossetia, one for Dagestan, and so on) and unite them under Umarov. However, the militant organizational structure had long been too broken to form any cohesive overarching group. Moreover, Umarov was not as charismatic or strong as past leaders. Infighting between the regional leaders quickly broke out, and the CE is now broken into countless groups all claiming to be the primary CE militant organization.

Fighting among the clans, among the militant organizations, and between the clans and militant organizations led the Kremlin to call the Second Chechen War complete by 2009. The declaration did not mean that the region would be stable or that terrorist attacks across Russia would cease. But those attacks mostly have been less organized and smaller in scale. Moreover, Moscow is no longer seriously threatened by the idea of the Russian Caucasus republics vying for independence.

Still, Moscow is not taking any chances by pulling its large military forces from the region. Instead, it is changing what those forces look like for the future. With the first and second Chechen wars, Russia placed a large military presence permanently in the Northern Caucasus. During the war, Russia moved nearly 100,000 troops into the region. At the end of the war, this has dramatically shifted — not only in number but also in the type of forces that are expected to keep peace in the region. Currently, Russian troops number approximately 50,000; another 40,000 Muslim (mainly Chechen) troops bring the total to 90,000.

The creation of ethnic Chechen brigades is a new concept — and one that is controversial in both the region and in Moscow. The Chechen brigades emerged from the tactic of pitting the clans and organizations against each other. The Russian military knew it would be easier for a Chechen force to understand what was needed on the ground for the day-to-day control of the regions. The ethnic Muslim brigades tend to use more brutal tactics that are not well received by the West though are sanctioned by the Kremlin. The Chechen brigades have received formal military training from the Russians, but are littered with reformed former militants. The Chechen brigades are headed by former militant and current Chechen President Ramzan Kadyrov and are mainly used to keep the peace in Chechnya, though they have expanded their reach to Ingushetia as well, despite the Ingush leadership's resistance. There is discussion in Moscow to create a similar military force in Dagestan, though without a clear leader in the republic to unite such forces it is an uncertain proposal for now.

The shift of responsibility for security in the region has dampened the violence as a whole, though instability persists. Russia understands that low-level conflicts will always remain in the republics. The larger concern is for the future of the region with the training, arming and organizing of ethnic forces into a functional military. Many in Moscow fear that this will lead to an ability to break away in the future, especially as the demographic balance between ethnic Russians and Muslims begins to tip.

CHAPTER 15:
The Future of the Caucasus

Barring the total direct and crushing occupation of the Caucasus by a single power — something STRATFOR does not see as likely within the next 15 years — the region will remain extraordinarily volatile. With that as the baseline, three major developments will shape the region over the next 15 years. Those developments are, in the order in which they will manifest: the Turkish-Persian contest for influence, the rise of Azerbaijan and the decline of Russia.

Turkish-Persian Competition over Mesopotamia

For the past decade, the United States has been almost wholly absorbed with events in the Middle East and South Asia. U.S. intelligence and foreign policy has been retooled to combat Islamist militancy, almost to the exclusion of all else, and the vast majority of deployable U.S. military ground forces have been on active duty in Iraq and Afghanistan. In the meantime, the world has slowly evolved.

After more than a few anxious moments, Russia has pulled itself back from the brink of dissolution and — with U.S. attention firmly riveted elsewhere — managed to re-create the security, political and economic foundation needed to survive as a reincarnated Russian empire. China, while remaining dependent upon the U.S.-designed and -maintained global trading system, has similarly undergone an internal political and economic consolidation. Iran has taken advantage of the Americans' smashing of Saddam Hussein's regime in Iraq to spread its influence into the Arab world. Each of these developments threatens long-term American interests far more than Islamist militancy, and over the next few years, the U.S. strategic position will adjust to reflect that.

The first U.S. position to be adjusted is Iraq, where the United States is in the final stages of slimming down from 130,000 soldiers to no more than 25,000. This will allow the United States to redeploy forces into more useful theaters, but it also sets the stage for the next regional conflict. With Iraq's power reduced, Iran sees an opportunity to dominate its traditional Mesopotamian rival decisively. Since the U.S. invasion in 2003, Iranian intelligence has been working to reshape Iraqi society and government into something Tehran can influence if not outright control. And with the American presence in Iraq dwindling, Iran is about to find out just how much influence it can wield in Iraq.

The major power most affected by this expansion of Persian power — other than Iraq, naturally — is not the United States but Turkey. Iranian control of Mesopotamia would represent a major shift in the balance of power between Persia and Anatolia that the Turks would not be able to tolerate. An Iranian-controlled Mesopotamia would expand the Iranian-Turkish border from a small, remote, uneventful stretch far from the Turkish core to a lengthy exposed area granting the Persians direct access to the now-expanded Turkish core in central Anatolia. It would also directly connect Iran and its ally Syria. Although neither Iran nor Syria alone could compete against committed Turkish power, the two together with Mesopotamia would comprise a force the Turks must reckon with. Such a competition would threaten not only Turkey's hoped-for geopolitical re-emergence but also Turkey's economic security, as Iraq is a key — and expanding — source of energy supplies for Turkey.

The only possible result of the American withdrawal, therefore, is a competition between Turkey and Iran over Mesopotamia.

That competition would take many forms and occur in many theaters. It would most likely involve competition in Lebanon, along with a more formalized series of Turkish military interventions into Iraqi Kurdistan. It might involve a Turkish military confrontation with

Syria. But most of Turkey's efforts will be focused upon Mesopotamia itself. Turkish success there would short-circuit any uniting of Syrian, Mesopotamian and Iranian power. Thus, Turkey will undoubtedly attempt to strengthen the Iraqi Sunnis' position in order to forestall Iranian supremacy. Competition over Iraq's energy assets will come into play.

For the Iranians, the key will be to keep Turks occupied elsewhere, attempting to distract them with events closer to home. That will lead to Persian agitation of the Kurds of both northern Iraq and southeastern Turkey. While Iran has its own Kurdish minority to worry about, it need not fear destabilization to the degree Turkey must. First, Iran's Kurdish minority is smaller than Turkey's (there are 5-8 million Kurds in Iran versus 15-20 million in Turkey). Second, Iran's internal social management structure is far more pervasive — and brutal — than Turkey's. Third, Iranian Kurds have been partially Persianized, making a Kurdish rebellion far less likely on Iran's side of the border. In contrast, the Kurds of Turkey clearly see themselves as a large, oppressed nation deliberately sidelined in the state in which they reside.

Iranian agitation of the Kurds is a threat that contemporary Turkey cannot ignore. Blocked from expansion into its traditional Danubian sphere of influence, Turkey's only option for near-term expansion is into Anatolia. A new Kurdish insurrection would threaten Turkish interests both short- and long-term, both at home and in its near abroad, both culturally and economically. Additionally, projecting power into Mesopotamia first requires that Turkey can reach Mesopotamia, and the only way to do that is through the heavily Kurdish-populated lands of southeastern Anatolia. Any Persian-Turkish competition in Mesopotamia almost by default will require Ankara gaining a far stronger grip in southeastern Anatolia than history would indicate is normally required. The stage is being set for a 1915-style contest, this time with the Persians rather than the Russians, and this time with the Kurds in the middle rather than the Armenians.

A broad Turkish-Persian competition has one major consequence for the Caucasus: The Turks and the Persians will both be largely occupied (with each other) elsewhere. Azerbaijan and Armenia may well emerge as a zone of competition between them, but considering how much higher the stakes are in Anatolia and Mesopotamia, any Turkish-Persian competition in the Caucasus will be one of proxy battles. Armenia's role as an occasional supplier or transit location for weapons to Iran may rise. At the most, this would see Turkey and Iran supply materiel and intelligence to Azerbaijan and Armenia, respectively — rather than participation in an outright war. This clash of core Turkish and Persian interests will certainly serve the interests of Russia, which wants to keep Turkey and Iran preoccupied.

The Rise of Azerbaijan

The American moment in the Caucasus has come and gone, but it left an artifact that is leading the region toward crisis: Azerbaijan's energy industry.

At the time of independence Azerbaijan was energy self-sufficient, with just enough excess oil production to earn a trickle of desperately needed income. The American presence in the 1990s, brief though it was, forced two developments: tens of billions of dollars of investment into the Azerbaijani energy industry and the construction of two parallel pipelines that carry Azerbaijani crude oil and natural gas to Turkey and the wider world without first going through either Russia or Iran. Taken together, Azerbaijani energy income has increased by a minimum of a factor of 20 between independence and 2011, and Azerbaijan's GDP has increased to approximately six times that of its rival Armenia. Considering that plans are already well advanced to produce additional volumes of oil and natural gas, the economic gap will only grow in the years ahead.

Azerbaijan is rising to a new level of power for an intra-Caucasus state, clearly leaving Armenia and Georgia far behind. While there is no risk of Azerbaijan rising to a level that can pose an existential threat to Iran, Russia or Turkey, all three powers are certainly viewing Azerbaijan in a very different light.

Baku obviously will find uses for its money, and one of those uses involves reclaiming territory it lost in the Nagorno-Karabakh war. While Azerbaijan's military spending has increased in recent years, the percentage of national wealth dedicated to defense has not. Yet in spending less than 5 percent of GDP on its military programs, Baku is still expected to reach a total defense budget of slightly more than $3 billion in 2012, an amount that dwarfs Armenia's expenditures by a seven-to-one ratio. It is reasonable to expect Azerbaijan to be spending more on its military annually than Armenia's GDP in about a decade. (This conservative estimate assumes no accelerated militarization effort from Baku.)

From Azerbaijan's point of view, the question is not if, but when to start a second Nagorno-Karabakh war. However, even with a growing and modernizing Azerbaijani military, many issues will prevent war from breaking out anytime soon. First, Nagorno-Karabakh is still a very difficult area in which to fight a war. Mountain enclaves do not fall easily to military power — a fact already familiar to Baku. The Azerbaijanis will not move until they feel confident of success.

Second, Baku understands that any war to reabsorb Nagorno-Karabakh also will be fought against Armenia. The constant flow of former Soviet military equipment and Armenian personnel support proved instrumental to Karabakh's success in the first war. Azerbaijan will be fighting an uphill battle — literally and figuratively — to dislodge Armenian power from the region.

Baku feels that it has control over both of these factors and that, as Azerbaijan gains more energy income, it will be able to overrun Armenian opposition in any stand-up fight. That may be true, but the Armenians will not be alone in the coming war, and Azerbaijani thinking at present is plagued by four massive miscalculations.

First, the Azerbaijani preoccupation with war with the Armenians flatly ignores the region's history. Never in the Caucasus' recorded history has any intra-Caucasus power been strong when even one of the major powers on the region's periphery has been powerful.

In all cases, the larger regional powers have either forced the intra-Caucasus powers into subordinate positions or simply eliminated any autonomy. Iran, Russia and Turkey all are on ascendant courses.

Second, Baku feels that while the interests of the larger powers may complicate and place some limits upon what Azerbaijan can do, in the end this is still only a fight between it and the Armenians. However, Armenia is not an independent state; it is a satellite that serves as the focus of Russian power south of the Greater Caucasus range. Russia currently has 5,000 soldiers in Armenia, including air and air defense forces, responsible for patrolling its borders with Azerbaijan, Georgia and Turkey. As part of the 2011 Armenian-Russian mutual defense treaty, the Russians have unlimited access to all Armenian territory and military infrastructure until 2044, with the military facilities at Yerevan, Gyumri and Erebuni seeing the most traffic. For comparison, the United States has never enjoyed that degree of freedom on any of its allies' territories unless it has directly occupied them. Essentially, Armenia is a Russian military base.

In many ways, Nagorno-Karabakh is just as vital to Russia's strategies as Armenia, because Nagorno-Karabakh's independence is the primary means used to seal Armenian cooperation. In the Nagorno-Karabakh war, Russian forces regularly leaked equipment and intelligence to Armenian forces, and Russian economic largess remains the single largest support mechanism for the Armenians of both Nagorno-Karabakh and Armenia proper. Even today, Karabakh's citizens eat Russian grain and use electricity generated and transmitted by infrastructure owned by Russian state-owned firms. Even more than Armenia, Nagorno-Karabakh is a proxy of the Russian state; it would not even exist if not for past Russian intervention and ongoing Russian support. Russia will no more allow a new Karabakh war to unfold without its participation than the Soviet Union would have allowed a Western invasion of Poland during the Cold War to proceed without it.

The Russo-Georgian war is a contemporary precedent for Russia acting proactively to destroy the military forces of a country it sees as threatening its proxies. Russian forces entered Georgia en masse within hours of the commencement of hostilities — something that could not have happened if Moscow had not coordinated with the South Ossetian provocation of Georgian forces. The war was engineered to serve Russia's purposes in general and secure a proxy's security specifically. From Russia's point of view, Nagorno-Karabakh and Azerbaijan could easily take the places of South Ossetia and Georgia in the script. This means that while another Nagorno-Karabakh war certainly is likely, hostilities could actually commence at the time and place of Moscow's choosing, rather than Baku's.

Azerbaijan's third miscalculation is not factoring in Iran. Tehran is nervous about the mere existence of an independent Azerbaijan on its northern border. Ethnic Azerbaijanis comprise one-quarter of Iran's population. From the Iranians' point of view, Azerbaijan luckily is not a liberal democracy with a vibrant independent press. Such a structure in Azerbaijan would do much to entice ethnic Azerbaijanis in Iran to resist Persian control. However, an authoritarian government in Baku obsessed with a military buildup to enable the reclamation of lost territory is not a significantly better development in Tehran's view.

The Persians' concerns are twofold. On one hand, they fear that should Baku succeed in retaking Nagorno-Karabakh and defeating Armenia, there will be no intra-Caucasus power left to balance Azerbaijan. Following the dictum that nothing encourages military action more than successful military action, the Persians fear that Azerbaijani attention would undoubtedly be redirected south, both because of the opportunity provided by the ethnic Azerbaijanis of Iran and the logic that there is no other reasonable direction for Azerbaijan to turn. In this scenario, Iran would be forced to intervene against Azerbaijan during the war or risk a larger confrontation later.

On the other hand, the Persians are well aware of the depth of the Russian relationship with Armenia and Nagorno-Karabakh — particularly since Iranian efforts to ingratiate themselves with the Armenians have met a wall of Russian resistance. Even greater than the Persian fear of a strong Azerbaijan is the Persian fear that Russia would take matters into its own hands and consolidate power in the Lesser Caucasus via a Georgia-style war.

But Baku's fourth and final miscalculation is perhaps the most dangerous. The Azerbaijanis believe that the possibility of Turkish involvement in a new Nagorno-Karabakh war would deter any possible Persian or Russian intervention. However, the Turkish-Azerbaijani "alliance" is one of the most misunderstood — and over-emphasized — relationships in the region. Ottoman Turkey ruled Azerbaijan for a shorter time than it ruled any of the other Ottoman territories — only 30 years (from 1590-1608 and 1724-1736). The Azerbaijanis accepted Turkish domination so freely that it has become ingrained in the Turkish mind that the Azerbaijanis are eager to re-enter the Turkish sphere of influence. But in the 275 years since the Turks ruled Baku, it has been ruled by other powers, most notably Persia and Russia — and the Azerbaijanis accommodated themselves to those powers nearly as easily as they did to Istanbul. When faced with invasion, the Azerbaijanis know they lack the insulation of the Georgians or the mountain fastnesses of the Chechens. For the Azerbaijanis limited resistance is a means to get a better vassalage agreement rather than an ideological stance; unlike the Chechens, the Azerbaijanis negotiate terms rather than continue to fight.

Simply put, the reality on the Azerbaijani side of the relationship simply does not match the expectations on the Turkish side. And as much as the Turks misunderstand the Azerbaijanis, the Azerbaijanis also misunderstand the Turks.

Turkey's economic past is in the natural extension of the waterways that end at Istanbul. The Danube and the Black Sea hold a wealth of possibilities for the Turks. Currently, those possibilities are locked under layers of political, economic and military arrangements that limit Turkish potential. Peeling those layers back will require constructive interaction with Europe and perhaps even Russia. Turkey is also on the verge of facing a major challenge from the Persians in Mesopotamia and will soon be forced to expend great efforts to prevent an ever more aggressive Iran from affecting core Turkish interests. Any Caucasus theater of that competition would be one of proxy conflicts, not outright war.

In dealing with challenges both in the European and Mesopotamian theaters, the last thing the Turks need is a war in the Caucasus, a region in which Turkish interests are thin and the potential for gains is so meager. But the greatest miscalculation the Azerbaijanis could make regarding Turkey is a lack of appreciation of Turkish history. Past Turkish expansion has favored targets that enhance Turkey's economic existence. This means that if Turkey went to war in the Caucasus in the modern age, it would be for energy. That would make Azerbaijan a target, not an ally.

Russian Twilight

There is no doubt that Russia is the dominant power in the region and will remain so for the next decade, but in the years that follow Russia faces challenges so dire that its presence in the intra-Caucasus region will all but disappear.

Russia's population is suffering a tremendous decline. The Russian birthrate collapsed at the end of the Soviet era, and while it has rebounded somewhat it still remains well below replacement level. The World Bank estimates that the Russian population will slip from 140 million in 2011 to somewhere in the 90-100 million range by 2050, and due to rising birth rates among non-Russian ethnicities in the Federation, ethnic Russians will only be a plurality of the population. There are roughly only half as many people in the 0-15 age group as there are in the 16-30 age group (21 million versus 41 million), so by 2020 Russia will begin suffering severe quantitative labor shortages.

Russia already has a massive qualitative shortage in its labor force, with wages for skilled labor in the St. Petersburg region already at or above the rates of Western metropolises like London or New York City. Moscow is slightly cheaper because it has been using the skilled labor forces from all of Russia's secondary population centers, but it will have depleted all of them within the next decade.

RUSSIAN DEMOGRAPHICS

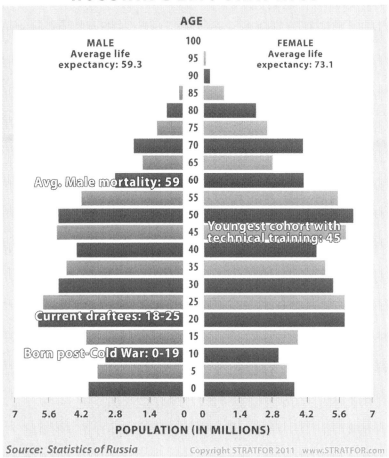

AGE

MALE
Average life
expectancy: 59.3

FEMALE
Average life
expectancy: 73.1

Avg. Male mortality: 59

Youngest cohort with technical training: 45

Current draftees: 18-25

Born post-Cold War: 0-19

POPULATION (IN MILLIONS)

Source: Statistics of Russia   Copyright STRATFOR 2011   www.STRATFOR.com

The problem is structural. As the Soviet Union edged toward collapse, one of the many ways in which it sought to conserve resources was by slimming down its technical education programs. Those programs largely collapsed during the Soviet dissolution. It is common for tertiary graduates in engineering and other technical fields in Russia to serve apprenticeships for several years before beginning their careers. Because of the collapse in the educational system, the youngest cadre of the population to have that level of education and experience is now aged 45. Officially, the average life expectancy for Russian males is 63, but it is probably much closer to 59 (the Russian census has been manipulated heavily for political purposes; Russian statistics have declared that the mortality age for men and women alike has increased by one year each year for the past four years, a statistical impossibility). By 2025, Russia will not have much of a skilled labor force at all. Considering the sheer surface area of the portions of Russia that are populated — to say nothing of those that are not — Russia simply will lack the labor force required to maintain its existing infrastructure, much less expand it.

Luckily for Moscow, Russia currently exists in a relatively benign security environment by Russian standards. Europe is also undergoing demographic decline (albeit at a much slower rate and with not nearly the degree of skilled labor shortages from which Russia suffers) and is unlikely to launch any wars of expansion in Russia's direction within the next decade. Central Asia and the Northern Caucasus have been reshaped into a formation fairly reminiscent of the old Soviet alignments. Ukraine is back under the Kremlin's watchful eye after a dalliance with pro-Western alignments. Even the Baltic states and Poland have moderated their opposition to all things Russian. While twilight is hardly imminent for the Russian nation, it is coming nonetheless. And as it arrives, the Russians will be forced to make a lengthy list of uncomfortable choices, with an eye toward delaying its own demise as long as possible. The Caucasus plays a central role in this, both in terms of hanging on until the last and knowing when to let go.

The past 300 years of Russian history has been about the search for physical barriers that can shield the Russians from exposure to potentially hostile powers. Since there are few barriers in Russia's surroundings more complete than the Greater Caucasus, withdrawal from this region will be one of the final acts of a dying Russia. By the time Russia pulls back from places like Grozny or Vladikavkaz it will have already withdrawn its dominating influence from Central Asia,

107

POPULATION IN NORTHERN CAUCASUS

COUNTRY	1990	2000	2010	2021*
Dagestan Republic	1,820,164	2,442,609	2,737,313	3,034,100
Republic of Ingushetia	189,340	340,028	516,693	611,600
Chechen Republic	1,100,334	1,110,237	1,268,042	1,607,900

*Projected
Source: Russian Federal Statistical Database

Siberia and Belarus. Perhaps only Ukraine, home to large volumes of steel and wheat production, not to mention a large Russian population, and an anchor in the Carpathians will remain in the Russian sphere of influence later than the Northern Caucasus republics.

The problem Russia will face is that its strategies for managing the Northern Caucasus are appropriate to the current period of relative Russian strength but not to the coming period of Russian demographic weakness. While the Russian ethnicity is among the fastest contracting populations in the Russian Federation, all of the Muslim ethnicities of the Caucasus are among the fastest growing — led by the Dagestanis, Chechens and Ingush.

Currently, Russia is empowering local Northern Caucasus groups, such as the Chechens, to keep each other in check. This has included training and arming Chechen battalions — now up to 40,000 in size — to handle security for Chechnya. The strategy is necessary, as it allows ethnic Russian forces to withdraw from the region and see to other areas of strategic concern to Moscow. Moscow's investments in the Caucasus are heavy, in per capita terms often more than is being sent to parts of core Russia, in order to undermine some of the economic grievances that can feed militancy. The Kremlin is so confident in the mid-term success of these ventures that it has planned the 2014 Olympics in Sochi — just 480 kilometers (about 300 miles) from Grozny. Many ski resorts, hotels and tourist destinations being planned or built will be located deep in the Caucasus, indicating the Russians are comfortable that they can prevent large security breaches for the next few years.

STRATFOR sees the period from 2011-2020 as being one of relative success for these policies, but it is a relatively short-term window of relative stability after decades of wars and failures. And more importantly — and ominously — in the longer term Russia's current Northern Caucasus policies are sowing the seeds of future crises.

First, the Kremlin has reignited competition between the republics. Since the Chechen security forces control their republic, they have been trying to extend their reach next door into Ingushetia. Since militancy exists across all of the republics, Grozny reasons that the Chechen battalions should be able to ignore Russia's internal borders and travel to wherever there is a need for security personnel. There are some in Moscow who share this view, and have allowed the Chechen security forces to cross over into Ingushetia for limited operations. However, this is controversial in Ingushetia. The two regions have been united in the past, so there is much overlap in infrastructure, culture, language and identity. However, Ingushetia has been separate from Chechnya for 19 years and has started to exhibit its own nationalist sentiment. The Ingush are starting to grow tired of their masters, both old and new.

The inter-republic tensions are even more intense with Dagestan, in which Moscow has wanted to replicate its ethnic battalion strategy. However, there is no real leader in the republic capable of uniting the main population, or at least forcibly controlling it, like Kadyrov in Chechnya. Kadyrov has offered his Chechen forces to oversee security in Dagestan, but that most likely would spark an immediate war between the republics. Memories are still too fresh in Dagestan (and in Moscow) of Chechnya's 1999 invasion that led to the Second Chechen War. But without an ethnic force to control Dagestan, and with Russian forces struggling in that republic and a strengthening Chechnya next door, this part of the region is a powder keg.

Right now, the Kremlin is attempting to keep the republics separate in order to keep their spats at a minimum. But that will last only so long. This leads to the next major issue: Kadyrov and his Chechen forces. The Kremlin has for the most part handed over security in Chechnya to Kadyrov, a man who has a great deal of experience in fighting the Russian state. Kadyrov's forces have since trained, organized and armed all his former militant associates and their children (who are now very capable fighters and leaders in their own right). The Russian state has essentially given the region all the tools it needs to rebel against Russian authority — up to and including a capable, authoritative, charismatic leader. For now, the Russian military could still defeat Chechen forces if needed, but in a decade or two when the Russian military faces crippling manpower limitations and the many children of the Chechen wars mature into fighters, it is difficult not to envision a new insurgency in the Northern Caucasus.

The strategy the Kremlin used to end the Second Chechen War and control the Caucasus currently is highly effective for when Russia is strong, but once the Russians' power declines it could well use up the rest of their resources. Russia's final years in the region are sure to be plagued by intense violence and likely a third Chechen war.

The intra-Caucasus region is a different story altogether. The Lesser Caucasus range is not nearly as formidable a barrier to movement as the Greater Caucasus, as they bleed into the highlands of both Anatolia and Persia at multiple points. As Iran and Turkey grow stronger — and become more competent due to mutual competition — Moscow will reach a point where the cost of its activities in the intra-Caucasus region exceeds the benefits, justifying a large-scale retreat to behind the Greater Caucasus.

STRATFOR expects Russia's intra-Caucasus region to be one of the first places the Russians leave. Of all of Russia's forward positions the intra-Caucasus region is the only one on the opposite side of one of Russia's strategic anchor points, and it is the only one where Russia is competing with multiple powers. Simply put, the position with the highest exposure, highest cost and lowest gain will be the first to be abandoned. So the question becomes, what will trigger that abandonment?

110

It will not be developments in Georgia, as Russia can maintain its position there quite easily. Russia is entrenched with small forces on the southern side of the Greater Caucasus, and those forces control the main access points into Georgia. Bereft of a powerful and dedicated foreign sponsor, Georgia is simply too weak and divided to cause any serious problems for the Russian position in the region, and since Russian intelligence has deeply penetrated the Georgian political system, it is not difficult for the Russians to detect and short circuit potential problems before they can fully manifest.

Azerbaijan is a more complicated situation, but it will not be what triggers the Russian retreat. The ethnic Azerbaijani population in Iran ensures that there will always be a major power interested in preventing Azerbaijan from becoming too powerful. The hostility of Nagorno-Karabakh and Armenia ensure that Azerbaijan will always have a military counterbalance (even if the balance is ever shifting in Baku's favor). And Russia is confident that even in the worst-case scenario of Azerbaijan launching a new Nagorno-Karabakh war, Moscow can easily use its own military to stop the Azerbaijanis cold.

The linchpin of the eventual Russian retreat centers on Armenia. Armenia lacks internal strategic planning capabilities — something Russia saw to very early in the post-Cold War era. The entirety of Yerevan's foreign policy effort is limited to soliciting the diaspora and any other interested groups for funds and keeping the topic of the events of 1915 alive. All of the serious policy planning is done in Moscow, not Yerevan. Contemporary Armenia is essentially a forward base of the Russian military. Should this position drag Armenia into a military conflict, or even drag Russia into conflict with Azerbaijan, Moscow has no serious concerns. But when Russia's position in Armenia threatens to drag Russia into a war with either Iran or Turkey, then the Russian position in Armenia will have outlived its usefulness. Both Iran and Turkey have far more positive demographics than Russia and are likely to face far fewer demands on their militaries (assuming that they can avoid war with one another). A fight in the intra-Caucasus region with either or both is not in Russia's interests, and so the abandonment of Armenia would be the most likely outcome. At that point there would be no fall-back position south of the Greater Caucasus, so abandoning Armenia to its fate means leaving the entire intra-Caucasus region to its own devices.

When this retreat occurs, it will be sudden and shocking. The Russian proxies and satellites of Abkhazia, Armenia, Nagorno-Karabakh and South Ossetia have only been able to secure and maintain their existence due to Russian largess. When the Russians leave, many of the de facto borders in the intra-Caucasus region will be up for grabs. This hardly means that Azerbaijan and Georgia will be able to fold wayward territories back into their states — although that is obviously one possibility. Rather, the freezing effect that Russia's strategic policies have imposed on the region will suddenly be lifted. And remember, the most likely scenario for the Russian withdrawal will be the rise of Iran or Turkey to such a point that they are willing to make a military bid for control of the intra-Caucasus region. There may be a moment when none of the big three powers is present, but it will only be a very brief one. Then the intra-Caucasus states will be dealing with a new master or set of masters.

Timeframes in this discussion are everything, and most of the goals of the Russian resurgence of the past decade have been explicitly geared toward pushing back the inevitable twilight. Overturning Ukraine's Orange Revolution re-anchored Russia in the Carpathians. Manipulating the Kazakh government and limiting the American footprint in Central Asia has re-anchored Russia in the Tien Shan Mountains. The Chechen and Georgian wars have solidified the Russian position in the Caucasus. With these forward positions secured, Russia can concentrate its shrinking manpower resources at specific points of vulnerability rather than spreading them out along a massive exposed border.

Economically, the Russian government is in the process of implementing a modernization program that aims to trade Western technology and capital for access to resources, a strategy that is the modern incarnation of Gorbachev's glasnost and perestroika, albeit with far less glasnost and a very tightly controlled perestroika. STRATFOR expects this modernization to fail in the long run — the obstacles to Russia's becoming an economically viable entity are simply too robust to be overcome with anything less than systemically-wrenching transformation — but in the short run we expect the effort to generate and regenerate a fair amount of Russian infrastructure and income streams. We project that this will enable the Russians to push back some of the financial aspects of their twilight, extending Russian strength for at least a few more years.

STRATFOR sees 2020-2025 as a major break point for the Russian Federation. At that point, the bottom will have fallen out of the Russian skilled labor pool and the dearth of births in the post-Cold War era will be affecting Russian military manpower. Additionally, Turkey and Iran will have had a decade to sort through internal restrictions on their great power aspirations, and both will be actively seeking new opportunities. Finally, the Americans will have most likely withdrawn sufficiently from the Islamic world that they will be able to consider in-force adventures into other regions. This collective pressure will most likely begin unraveling the Russian position in the intra-Caucasus region.

But while the Russians are likely to abandon Armenia quickly, they will hold on as long as they can to the area north of the Greater Caucasus range. As much as the Russians will not want to seek combat with rejuvenated and expanding Iran and Turkey, they know that simply walking away from the Greater Caucasus would invite foreign penetration into their core territories. Even weakened, Russia should be able to maintain its anchor in the Greater Caucasus for years — and likely decades — before being dislodged. It will be a violent occupation, particularly once Iran and/or Turkey begins agitating the North Caucasus populations against Russian rule, but that occupation will play to most of the strengths in the Russian system. In the years following Russia's withdrawal from the intra-Caucasus region, Russia is likely to face similar pressures in Northern Europe, Siberia, Central Asia and Ukraine, likely in that order. But the Russians likely will retain the strength necessary to maintain their grip on the Northern Caucasus until their decline.

Put simply, Russia's demise is most likely to start in the Caucasus, and it is most likely to end there as well.

CONCLUSION:
A Path for the United States

We have considered two layers of the Caucasus. The first layer consists of the intra-Caucasus nations of Armenia, Azerbaijan and Georgia. The second layer is the great powers of Iran, Russia and Turkey. Each of these has interests in the Caucasus as well as in other regions.

But there is a third layer as well: that of global powers that irregularly penetrate into the region. The only one of those that exists these days is the United States. The United States has global interests and engages each of the three great regional powers directly on a range of issues. Most of these have nothing directly to do with the Caucasus. It is through this framework of non-Caucasus issues that the United States interacts with the intra-Caucasus states — and those relations are never bilateral. They always intersect with the regional powers and are frequently shaped by them.

For example, there is no such thing as stand-alone U.S.-Georgian relations. Instead, U.S.-Georgian relations are embedded within U.S.-Russian relations. Relations with Georgia are not simply conditioned by relations with Russia; they cannot be understood without that context. Similarly, U.S. relations with Armenia are conditioned by relations with Turkey and Russia as well as by domestic American politics, since Armenian-Americans represent a large constituency in the United States that shapes U.S. policies toward the region. U.S.-Azerbaijani relations are perhaps the most complex, shaped by U.S. relations with Turkey, Russia and Iran, as well as with Armenia and Georgia.

With indirect — rather than direct — interests shaping U.S. involvement in the Caucasus, U.S. relationships with the three intra-Caucasus countries are shaped by those countries' relations with the larger regional powers, as well as their relations with each other and with other nations outside the region. This is a constantly shifting foundation, which means U.S. relations with Armenia, Azerbaijan and Georgia are inherently unstable. From the standpoints of Baku, Tbilisi and Yerevan, Washington conducts a highly unpredictable and inexplicable policy in the region. It is a constant complaint from Georgia in particular, which is perhaps closest to the United States, that it is difficult to get and keep the attention of the United States or to predict long-term relations with it.

This is an accurate view of the situation. The American relationship with these countries ultimately depends on issues not rooted in the region and typically only indirectly involving the region. The intra-Caucasus states are unable to focus U.S. efforts on their interests unless it intersects other, more important interests. Georgia's relative success at attracting American interest has less to do with Georgia and more to do with U.S. strategy regarding Russia, a strategy that currently is defunct. The relative cool relationship with Azerbaijan is less about Baku and more that the Americans do not see Azerbaijan's relations with Russia and Iran as significantly affecting the U.S. position. U.S. relations with Armenia focus on atmospherics driven by domestic politics but are ultimately defined by Armenia's close relations to Russia and trading relations with Iran. None of the U.S. relationships with the three small Caucasus states stands on its own merits.

It follows that without understanding U.S. strategy in general, it is impossible to understand U.S. policies in the Caucasus. The United States first ventured into the region just after World War II and has had three strategies since then.

From the declaration of the Truman Doctrine until the collapse of the Soviet Union in 1991, the United States followed the strategy of containment, designed to prevent the Soviets from expanding beyond the limits reached by the Red Army in 1945. At the heart of the Truman Doctrine was the desire to stabilize Greece and Turkey. Turkey in particular was central to U.S. global policy, as the Bosporus was the Soviet gateway to the Mediterranean, where the Soviets had acquired clients in Egypt and Syria. Maintaining control of the Bosporus required a stable Turkey. The United States did not have ambitions to move north into the Caucasus, seeing Armenia, Azerbaijan and Georgia completely embedded in the Soviet Union. It was content to hold the Turkish-Soviet line in the Lesser Caucasus as a frozen border. It is interesting that when the Iranian revolution occurred in 1979, one of the key interests was that Iran would maintain its position south of Azerbaijan and block the Soviets. The United States did not need a friendly Iran to achieve its strategic goal of containing the Soviets. Islamic Iran holds its position in the Caucasus just as well as the Shah's Iran, and in this theater at least it continues to serve U.S. interests nicely.

The second phase began in 1991 and ended in 2008. This was a period in which the former Soviet states were finding their way, at times violently, while the Russian Federation was first floundering and later finding its balance. The United States adopted two contradictory strategies. Deeply concerned about the future of the Soviet nuclear arsenal and disturbed by the idea of several nuclear powers emerging from the Soviet wreckage, the United States supported Russia's claim that it was the Soviet Union's sole successor. At the same time, the United States wanted to develop a system of bilateral relationships with other former Soviet republics, first implicitly and later explicitly with the intent of expanding NATO. From the American point of view, the strategy was benign. But on a deeper level, following the long, bitter Cold War, the United States was obviously not eager to see Russia reassert itself. The strategy of engaging former Soviet republics in military relationships made sense.

The Russians were deeply uneasy about this dual strategy in the 1990s. Some feared that it represented a new containment strategy. But what they thought mattered little, inasmuch as the Russians were unable to resist the United States. NATO expanded into Central Europe and made clear that it would admit the Baltic states — which had been republics of the USSR — soon enough. Whatever the subjective intentions of the United States, the objective appearance to the Russians was one of a resurrection and an extension of containment — something the Russian Federation could not survive. But the critical point was that the United States thought it had ample time to execute both of its strategies.

The U.S.-Turkish relationship remained solid during that period, and Iran had not yet emerged as a major problem for the United States. The American focus in the Caucasus was limited to Russia, which was fighting a war in Chechnya that tied it down. The American relationship with Georgia potentially blocked Russian expansion and increased Russian insecurity by allowing the Chechens a back door for gaining supplies through Georgia. The United States was relatively indifferent to the Armenian-Azerbaijani war, content to focus on Georgia as part of its broader strategy of separate bilateral relations. Nor did it over-concern itself with the security of Georgia, judging that Russia was in no position to challenge it.

The third phase occurred in stages: with the rise of Vladimir Putin, with the 9/11 attacks and finally solidifying with the August 2008 Russo-Georgian war.

Putin was not simply a strong leader. His rise led directly to the reinvigoration of the Russian intelligence apparatus. With that apparatus, Russia could begin ruling itself again, and as that apparatus consolidated itself in the halls of the Kremlin, it could again begin reaching out to former Russian territories. It was unclear whether the Russian intelligence apparatus would have the room it needed to consolidate — at least until al Qaeda attacked the United States on Sept. 11, 2001.

The Americans became concerned that al Qaeda would be able to do exactly as it promised — band the entire Islamic world into a single, gigantic power that could challenge the American position. Combating that perceived threat made the United States' Russian strategy a subsidiary interest. The United States focused its efforts overwhelmingly on the Islamic world, first invading Afghanistan and then Iraq. This did not mean that the United States abandoned its Russian strategy. It merely put it on autopilot, continuing to build relationships in the former Soviet Union while maintaining strong relations with Russia, which was helping with U.S. efforts in Afghanistan. This shift in Washington's focus allowed the Russian intelligence apparatus to heal, consolidate and grow.

These disparate trends generated a crisis in U.S.-Russian relations. The logic of the American strategy led to supporting the Orange Revolution in Ukraine, which gave rise to a government that the Russians perceived as being created by U.S. intelligence specifically to serve as a fundamental threat to Russian national security. Russian strategy shifted greatly. Moscow now publicly stated that Washington was engaged in an attempt to destroy the Russian Federation and took steps to reverse the trend.

The United States, completely committed militarily to the Middle East, did not have the resources to take or maintain an aggressive stance in the former Soviet Union. At the same time, it did not shift its behavior. The issue came to a head in the Caucasus, where Russia became increasingly hostile toward Georgia, a country isolated because of American preoccupation elsewhere. The Russians wanted to demonstrate that U.S. guarantees were worthless, a message primarily for consumption by Ukraine, the Baltic states, and other former Soviet republics. In 2008, after complex maneuvers on both sides, Russia attacked Georgia. The purpose was not to occupy Georgia as much as to humiliate the United States and demonstrate its weakness. Russia's interest was not in the Caucasus per se, but the Caucasus provided the opportunity to drive home the lesson.

The August 2008 war fully pushed the Americans into a new Caucasus strategy. It can best be described as strategic confusion. In short, U.S. relations with all three of the larger powers with interests in the Caucasus are in such flux that it is difficult to craft policies toward them, much less the intra-Caucasus states.

Relations with Iran deteriorated dramatically as the U.S. position in Iraq weakened. Relations with Turkey, strained by Ankara's refusal to cooperate in Iraq in 2003, deteriorated as the United States perceived Turkey as increasingly hostile. U.S. relations with Russia superficially improved in 2009, but the mutual wariness remained in place.

Without guiding policies toward the three regional powers, U.S. relations with the intra-Caucasus powers have become particularly erratic. In Georgia, the Americans are planning to build a Georgian military that can resist Russia without massive American reinforcement (it is a dubious possibility, but it is the policy nonetheless). The United States attempted to pull Armenia out of the Russian sphere of influence by pressuring Turkey on the Armenian genocide issue. This won little favor in Armenia — which signed a treaty with Russia allowing it to maintain forces there through 2044 — while alienating Turkey. And the United States continued being wary of entanglement with Azerbaijan.

The United States' apparent incoherence in the region derives from two factors. One we have already addressed: The United States does not see the region as a core interest in itself. Second, and more immediate, is that the American preoccupation with the Islamic world has led to a lack of resources and attention needed to engage such a complex region.

Still, when we consider American issues in the region, there is a natural evolution that could take place. Hostilities between the United States and Iran could be somewhat settled by negotiations, but even then relations would not be stable. The United States needs time to clarify its relationship with Turkey. And the United States does not want to disengage from confronting Russia as it wants to limit Russia's advance on as many fronts as possible. For both geopolitical and psychological reasons, Washington does not want to see Georgia occupied and linked to Armenia, and the United States wants to maintain an alternative supply line to Afghanistan independent of both Russia and Pakistan — a safety net.

In order for any of these issues to be addressed, the key U.S. relationship must be with Azerbaijan. First, supporting the Georgian position is made easier by far with a cooperative Azerbaijan, which is now the strongest country of the intra-Caucasus trio. Second, a presence in Azerbaijan creates a threat to Iran that could make Tehran more open to settlement of outstanding issues elsewhere. Third, the alternative supply line to Afghanistan would be the trans-Caspian route that runs through Azerbaijan.

Obviously, Azerbaijan by itself is not enough. The United States needs Georgia, for without Georgia Azerbaijan is landlocked and unreachable. The United States also must mend its relationship with Turkey, not because they agree with each others' policies but because the United States needs Turkey to counterbalance Iran (and perhaps Russia), and in the end Turkey needs the United States if it is to develop into the dominant regional power it wants to be. A Turkish-Azerbaijani bloc would be a logical geopolitical outcome.

But it is an outcome that carries a price. Georgia cannot stand on its own, or really even with the indirect support the U.S. has been sending. It needs to be sufficiently well armed to be able to deter Russian military action. That will require a level of military commitment from the Americans that heretofore they have been unwilling to consider for fear of being drawn into a conflict in which they have no direct stakes.

In order to secure Azerbaijan and Turkey, the United States must side against Armenia, and do that from the Turkish and Azerbaijani point of view. This would create no major problems for Turkey, as the Turks are broadly fine with the status quo. For Azerbaijan, it carries a major price: helping to find a solution to Nagorno-Karabakh, against Armenia's desire to maintain the status quo. This is undertaking a substantial — and perhaps military — burden in order to achieve a position in the region that satisfies a series of geopolitical needs.

The alternative for the United States is to abandon Georgia as too distant and isolated to support, which does more than simply damage U.S. credibility throughout the former Soviet Union. Abandoning Georgia writes off any possibility of a strategic relationship with Azerbaijan, which means no backup route to Afghanistan, no lever against Iran and a weakening of the long-term relationship with Turkey.

Abandoning the region is not an existential loss. The United States would survive the loss of its Georgian client, it can live without

Turkey, and even should Iran and Russia solidify their regional dominance life would go on in America. But such losses are not trivial and ultimately not necessary. The costs of a Turkey-Azerbaijan-Georgia bloc are relatively low financially and politically, and the advantage that could be gained against Iran and/or Russia substantial.

Nations normally pursue their national interest, and that is no different for the United States. But unraveling its position in the Islamic world and refocusing on future challenges would not be easy for any country and certainly not for the United States, which tends to turn inward after wars.

The American position in the region is weak, overshadowed as it is by concerns elsewhere. But there is most certainly an opportunity in the Caucasus that would allow a strengthening of the American position not just in the Middle East, but in the former Soviet Union as well. The evolution of this policy will be measured in years rather than months, and there is always the possibility that Russia or Iran will move preemptively and eliminate that opportunity.

It is precisely that preemptive threat, particularly from Iran, that makes this series of relationships so significant. The United States needs Turkey as a counterweight to Iran. The United States needs Georgia as a demonstration of its will. The United States needs Azerbaijan as its linchpin.

The Caucasus itself will never be a centerpiece of American strategy. But the regional powers on its periphery are always important to Washington. If it is to manage those powers, the United States must allow itself to be drawn more deeply into the Caucasus. Azerbaijan is the next, key move.

Dr. George Friedman
Founder and CEO
STRATFOR
Austin, Texas
May 20, 2011

Made in the USA
Columbia, SC
15 June 2023